Thank you...

... for purchasing this copy of **Wet Play Today for ages 7-9**. We hope you find it useful on those wet days when the children need occupying inside at break and playtimes.

Please note that photocopies can only be made for use by the purchasing institution. Supplying copies to other schools, institutions or individuals breaches the copyright licence. Thank you for your help in this.

This Wet Play Today book is part of our growing range of educational titles. Most of our books are individual workbooks but, due to popular demand, we are now introducing a greater number of photocopiable titles especially for teachers. You may like to look out for:

WET PLAY TODAY for ages 5-7, 7-9, 9-11

READING FOR LITERACY for Reception and for ages 5-7, 7-8, 8-9, 9-10, 10-11

WRITING FOR LITERACY for ages 5-7, 7-8, 8-9, 9-10, 10-11

SPELLING FOR LITERACY for ages 5-7, 7-8, 8-9, 9-10, 10-11

NUMERACY TODAY for ages 5-7, 7-9, 9-11

HOMEWORK TODAY for ages 5-7, 7-8, 8-9, 9-10, 10-11

BEST HANDWRITING for ages 4-7, 7-11

To find details of our other publications, please visit our website: **www.acblack.com**

Contents

Contents

Number Crosswords

Work out the answers to the clues to fill in the grid.
Use a pencil in case you make a mistake.

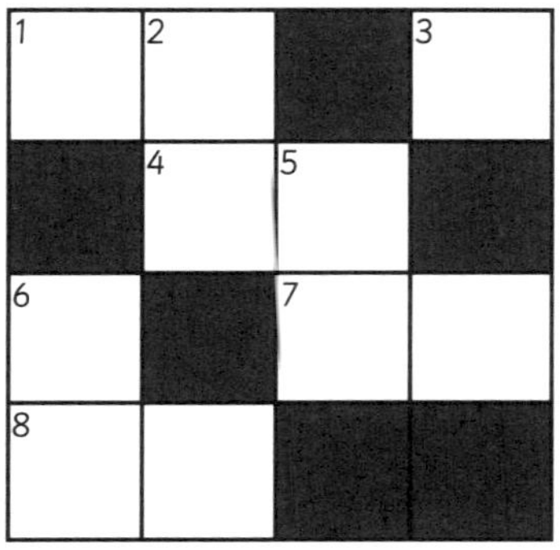

Across

1. 12 + 12
3. 6 + 3
4. 30 + 35
7. 20 + 30
8. 15 + 15

Down

2. 45 + 1
5. 45 + 10
6. 6 + 7

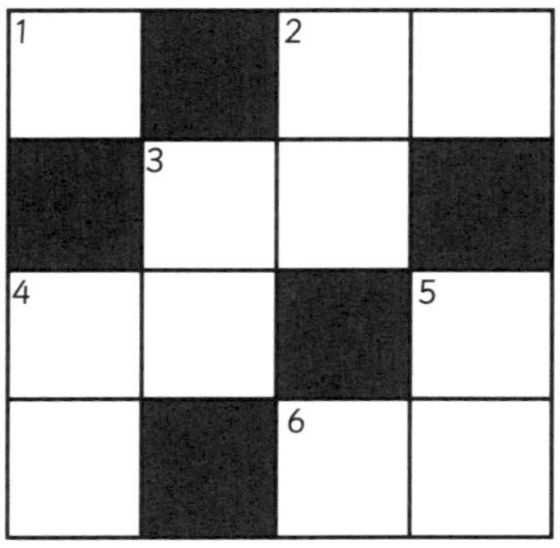

Across

1. 2 + 0
2. 6 + 6
3. 60 + 4
4. 70 + 3
6. 24 + 3

Down

2. 7 + 7
3. 33 + 30
4. 40 + 30
5. 8 + 9

Across

1. 100 + 25
3. 310 + 5
5. 74 + 10
6. 16 + 3
8. 50 + 50

Down

1. 7 + 4
2. 15 + 10
3. 20 + 19
4. 440 + 400
6. 5 + 5
7. 50 + 40

Number Crosswords - Answer Sheet

(1) 2	(2) 4	■	(3) 9
■	(4) 6	(5) 5	■
(6) 1	■	(7) 5	0
(8) 3	0	■	■

Across

1. 12 + 12 = 24
3. 6 + 3 = 9
4. 30 + 35 = 65
7. 20 + 30 = 50
8. 15 + 15 = 30

Down

2. 45 + 1 = 46
5. 45 + 10 = 55
6. 6 + 7 = 13

(1) 2	■	(2) 1	2
■	(3) 6	4	■
(4) 7	3	■	(5) 1
0	■	(6) 2	7

Across

1. 2 + 0 = 2
2. 6 + 6 = 12
3. 60 + 4 = 64
4. 70 + 3 = 73
6. 24 + 3 = 27

Down

2. 7 + 7 = 14
3. 33 + 30 = 63
4. 40 + 30 = 70
5. 8 + 9 = 17

■	(1) 1	(2) 2	5	■
(3) 3	1	5	■	(4) 8
9	■	■	(5) 8	4
■	(6) 1	(7) 9	■	0
(8) 1	0	0	■	■

Across

1. 100 + 25 = 125
3. 310 + 5 = 315
5. 74 + 10 = 84
6. 16 + 3 = 19
8. 50 + 50 = 100

Down

1. 7 + 4 = 11
2. 15 + 10 = 25
3. 20 + 19 = 39
4. 440 + 400 = 840
6. 5 + 5 = 10
7. 50 + 40 = 90

Dinosaur Grid

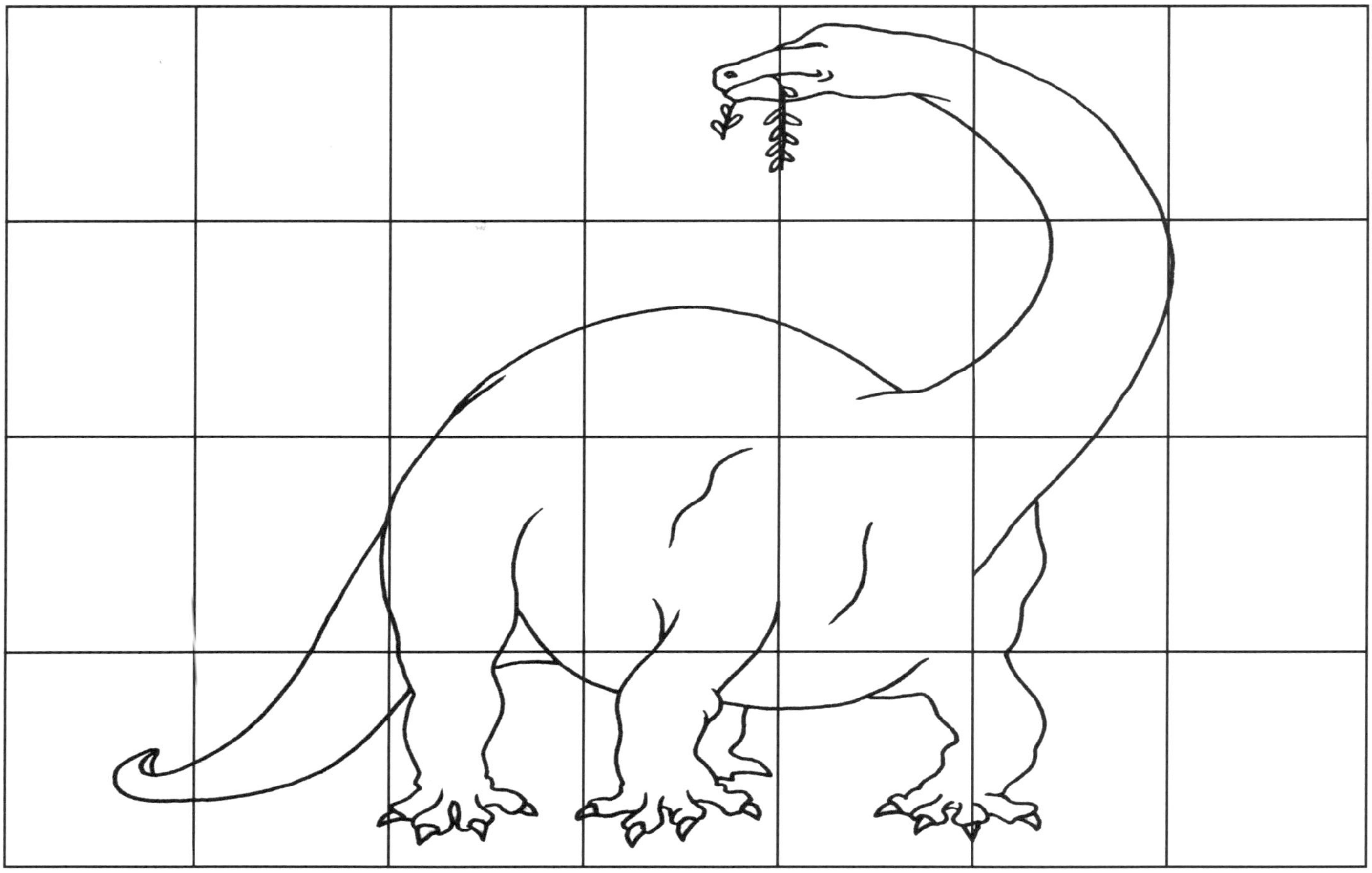

Copy the picture into the grid. Try to copy one square at a time.

Jungle Animals

Find and colour:

1 monkey 

2 fish 

3 birds 

4 frogs 

5 leaves like this one: 

6 flowers like this one: 

Who's Behind the Tree?

Find the right route through the maze and then write the letters you find on the route in the space below to find out what is hiding behind the tree.

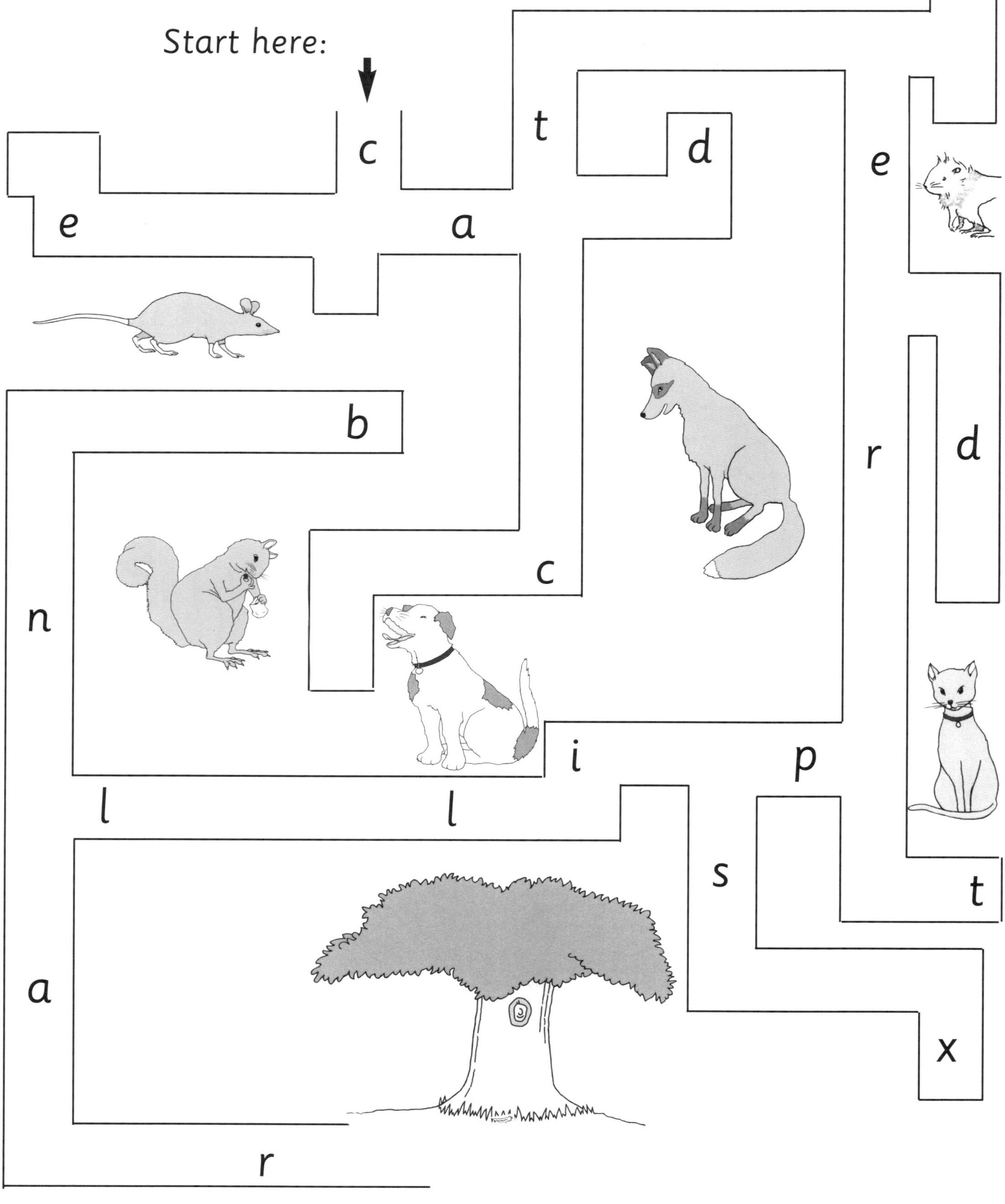

_ _ _ _ _ _ _ _ _ _ _

Jungle Safari

You are exploring a dense jungle. Suddenly you hear a movement ahead of you.
You look through your binoculars and see …………
Draw what you can see through your binoculars.

Alphabet Fun

You can play this on your own or as a competition with a friend. Choose any letter of the alphabet and then try to think of something that fits into each subject group shown below.
When you have filled in as much as you can with one letter, try again with a different letter.

Subject group	**First choice**	**Second choice**	**Third choice**
Animal			
Vegetable			
Country			
Boy's name			
Girl's name			
Flower			
Food			
Fruit			
Football team			
Book title			
Pop group			
Bird			
Vehicle			

What's Hidden in the Garden?

Sort out the jumbled words to make the names of plants.

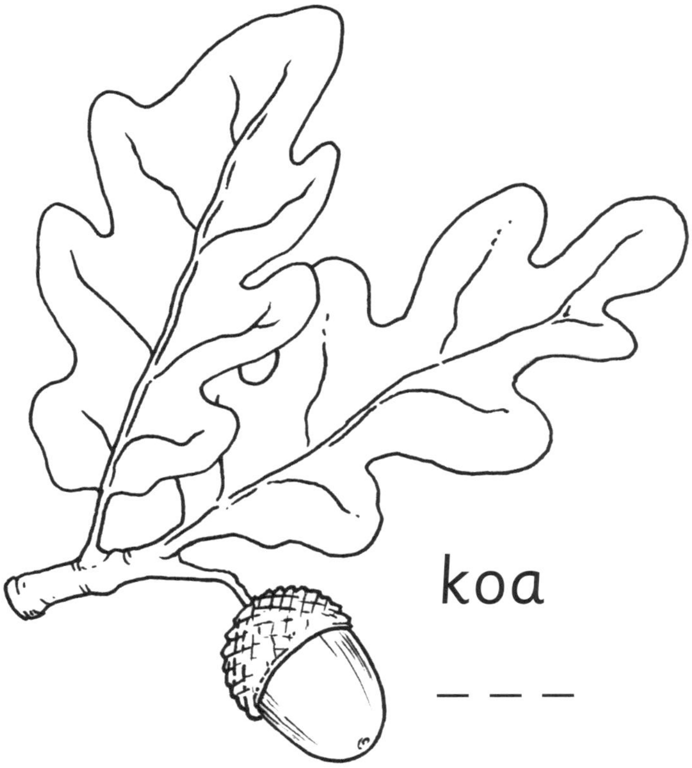

koa

_ _ _

ylohl

_ _ _ _ _

adsyi

_ _ _ _ _

ucsrco

_ _ _ _ _ _

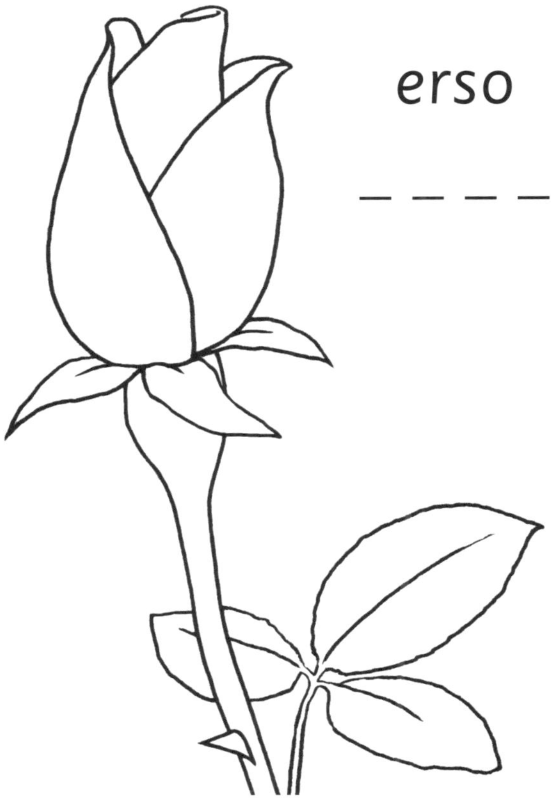

erso

_ _ _ _

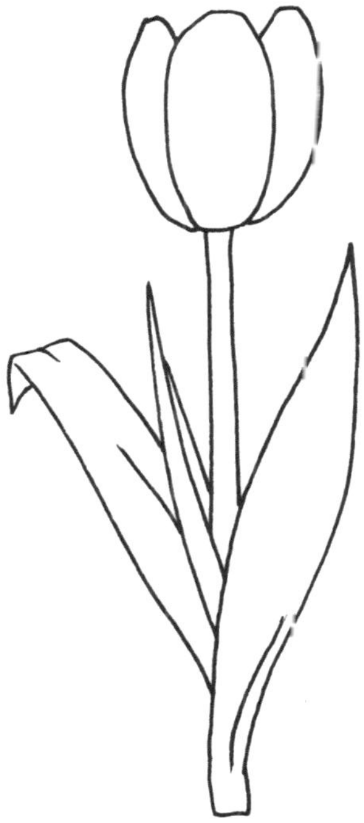

pilut

_ _ _ _ _

Now colour the pictures.

Snake

Colour in the patterns on the snake
and then cut along the lines.
Tie a piece of cotton through the
head to see it squirm about.

Sport Wordsearch

c	a	p	w	x	g	o	a	l
r	b	t	p	o	o	l	s	c
o	u	z	o	f	j	y	w	b
w	h	i	s	t	l	e	x	p
d	n	j	t	m	t	o	z	n
f	y	p	w	i	g	a	m	e
b	a	l	l	x	j	w	u	t
a	d	s	z	c	r	u	n	b
t	b	t	e	a	m	j	f	a

Words to find:

1. whistle
2. goal
3. game
4. net
5. post
6. crowd
7. ball
8. bat
9. team
10. cap
11. pool
12. run

Number Sequences

Find these sequences of numbers and put a circle around them. Be sure to look carefully as they might be horizontal, vertical, diagonal or even backwards.

1765	132	817
248	5430	39
671	597	188
901	459	918
	25	280
		399

5	2	6	9	0	1	8
4	7	1	0	5	3	4
3	3	6	8	4	2	7
0	1	7	6	5	6	1
6	0	1	1	9	8	1
2	4	8	5	7	9	3
9	1	8	2	0	4	3

Find some more sequences of numbers and write them out for your friend to find.

Finish the Picture

Colour the picture and draw in the missing parts where the arrows tell you.

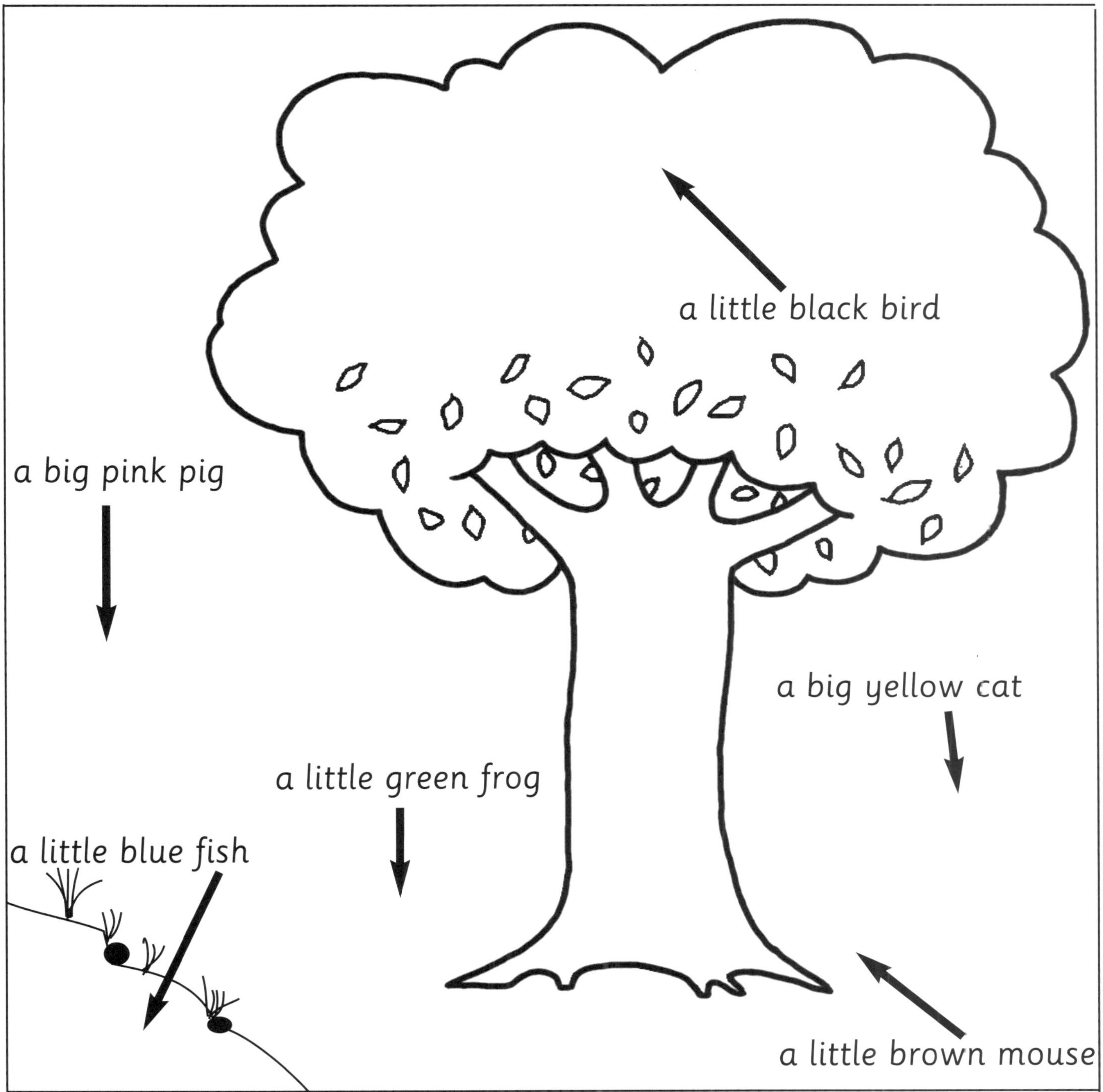

 pig

 bird

 cat

 fish

 mouse

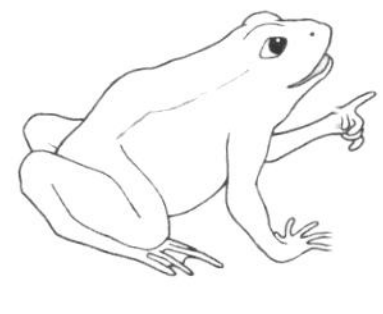 frog

Paper Star

You will need 5 sheets of paper from a colour magazine.

✶ Roll up each sheet of paper into a long 'straw'. Start with the long side and roll as tightly as you can.

✶ Tape the 'straw' to stop it coming undone.

✶ Use elastic bands or tape to make two 'v' shapes, see diagram 1.

✶ Weave these together, see diagram 2, and tape where the straws cross.

✶ Complete the star by weaving the fifth straw in and taping it firmly.

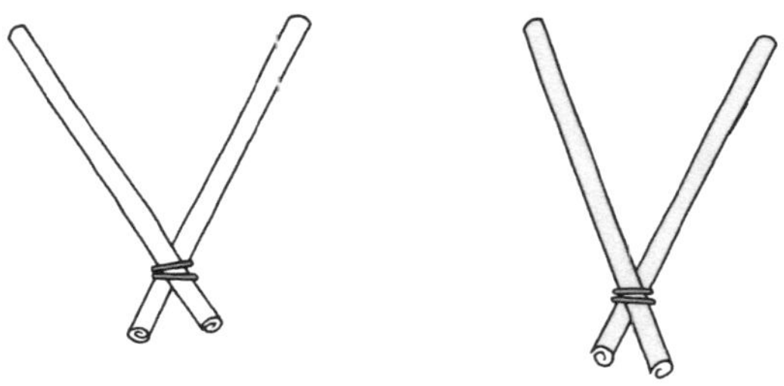

diagram 1

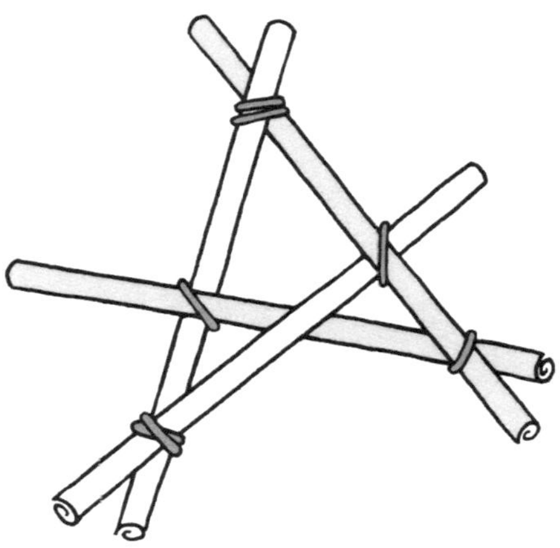

diagram 2

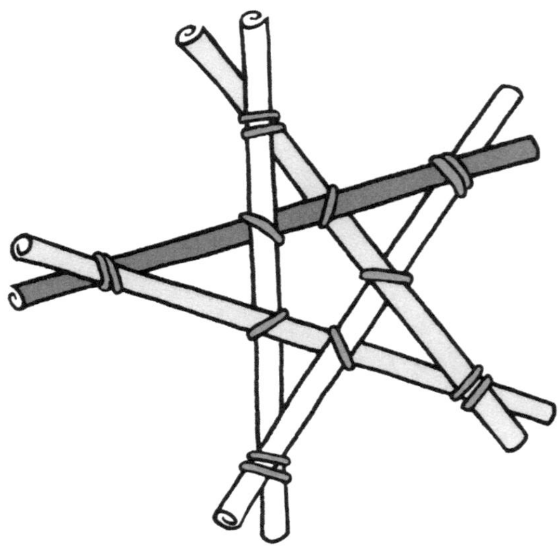

diagram 3

Fantasy Tree

❊ Roll a double sheet of newspaper (or coloured paper) into a tight tube. Roll from the short end.

❊ Tape one end of the roll so that the roll does not undo on its own.

❊ Cut narrow strips down the tube to within 10cm of the tape. You must keep cutting until all the paper is made into strips.

❊ Bend the strips down and then carefully pull upwards from the centre.

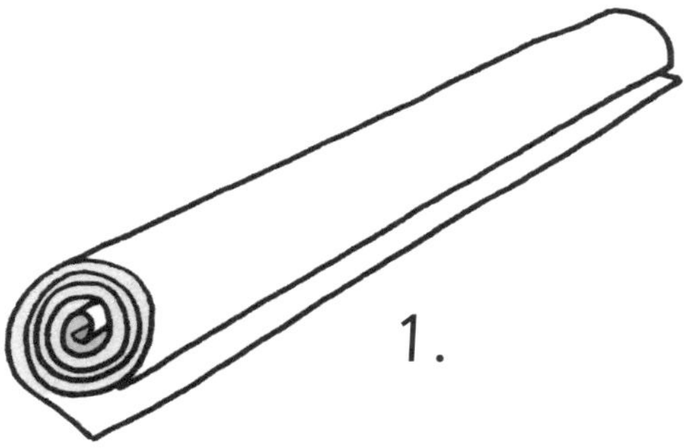

1.

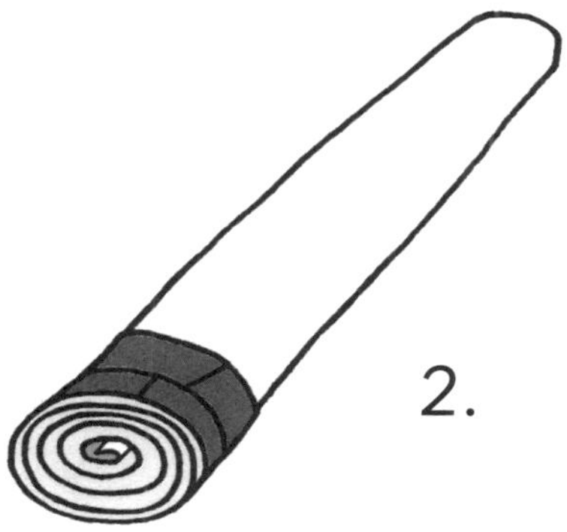

2.

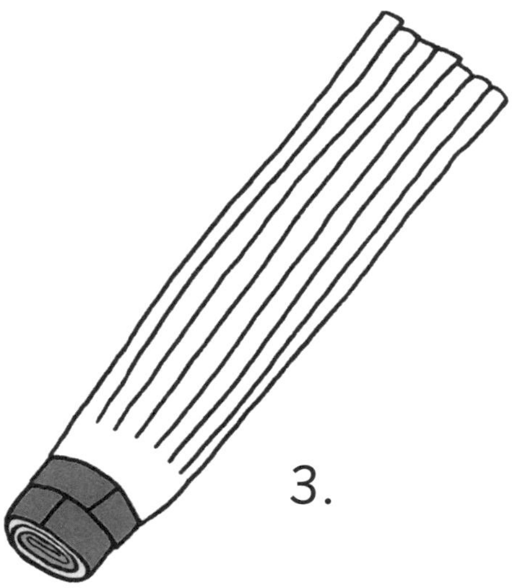

3.

4.

Circus Clowns

❇ Colour in all the clowns.

❇ Cut along the solid lines to make two strips.

❇ Fold each strip along the dotted lines into a concertina.

❇ Cut out the clowns making sure you leave the hands joined.

❇ Open out the strips and join them together with tape.

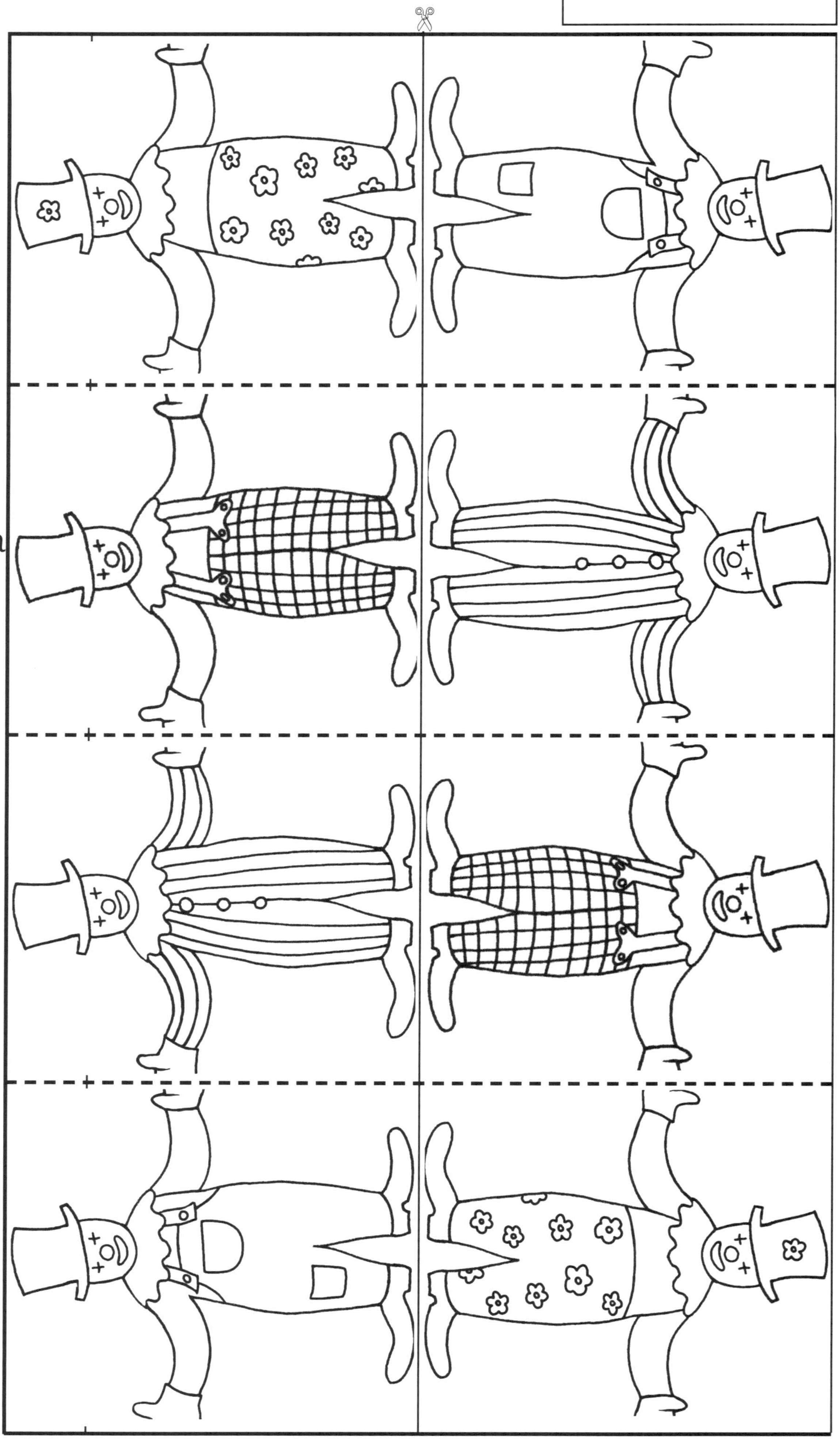

Paper Beads

✤ Colour all the triangular shapes, then cut them out.

✤ Starting at the large end, carefully roll up the strip, quite tightly but without squashing your bead.

✤ Glue the pointed end down and hold until it is stuck.

✤ You have now made one bead, repeat with the other shapes.

✤ You could use the triangular shape as a template and make your beads out of coloured magazines.

✤ When you have made all your beads, get someone to help you thread them up with a needle and strong cotton or shirring elastic.

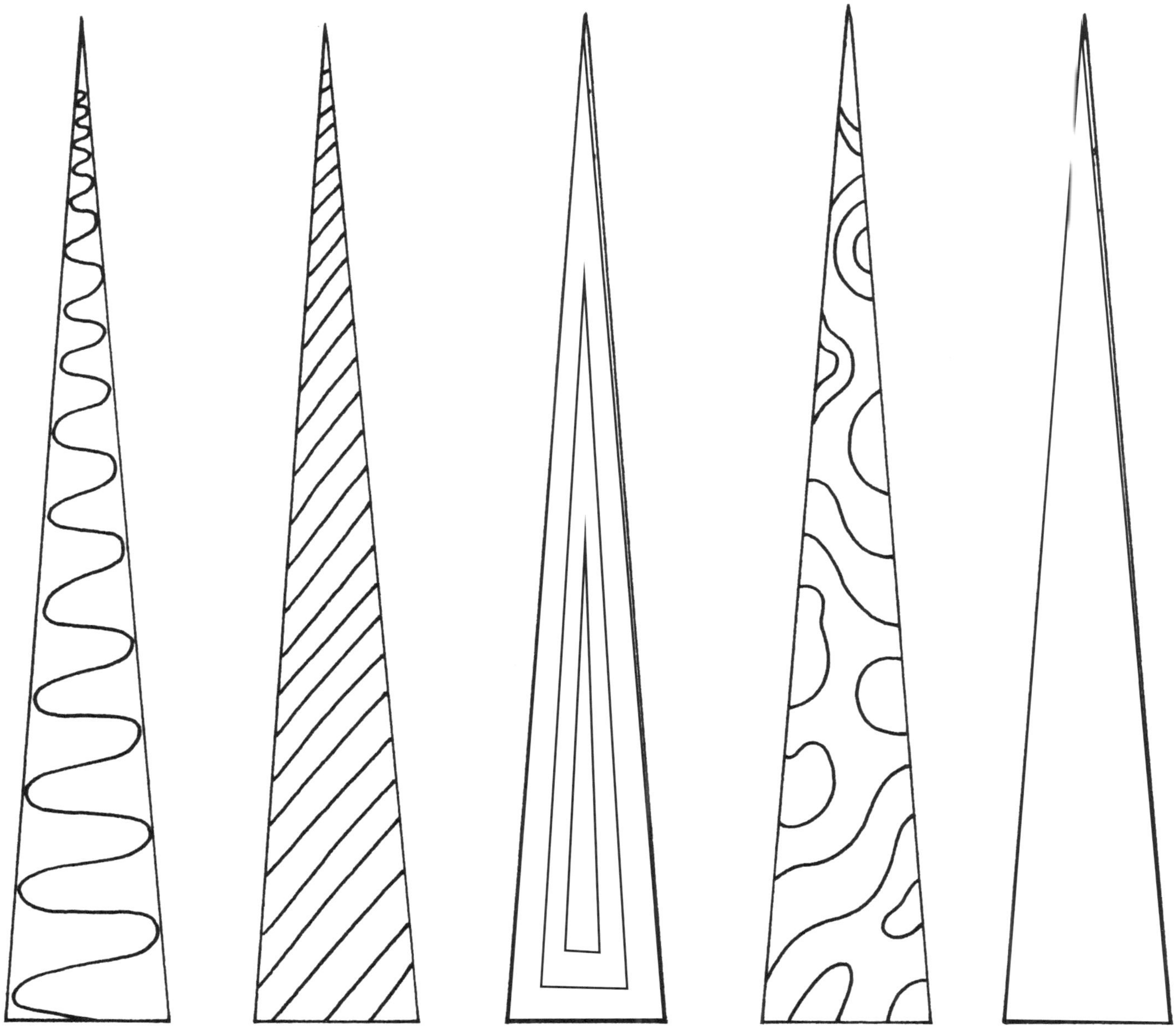

Paper Lantern

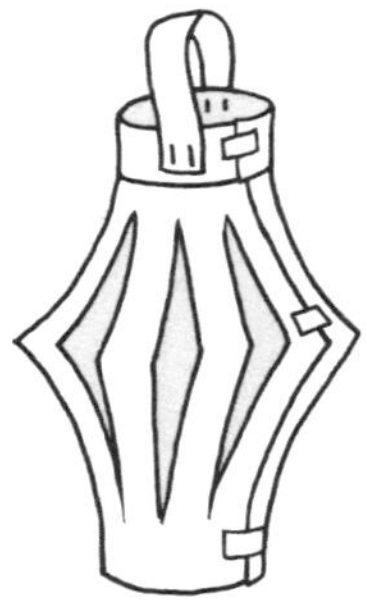

1. Colour in all of the oblong.
2. Cut the oblong out and fold along the fold line.
3. Cut from the fold as far as the solid line.
4. Open out the oblong and bend it round.
5. Paste one edge over the other.
6. Use the remaining strip to make a handle and stick it across the top.

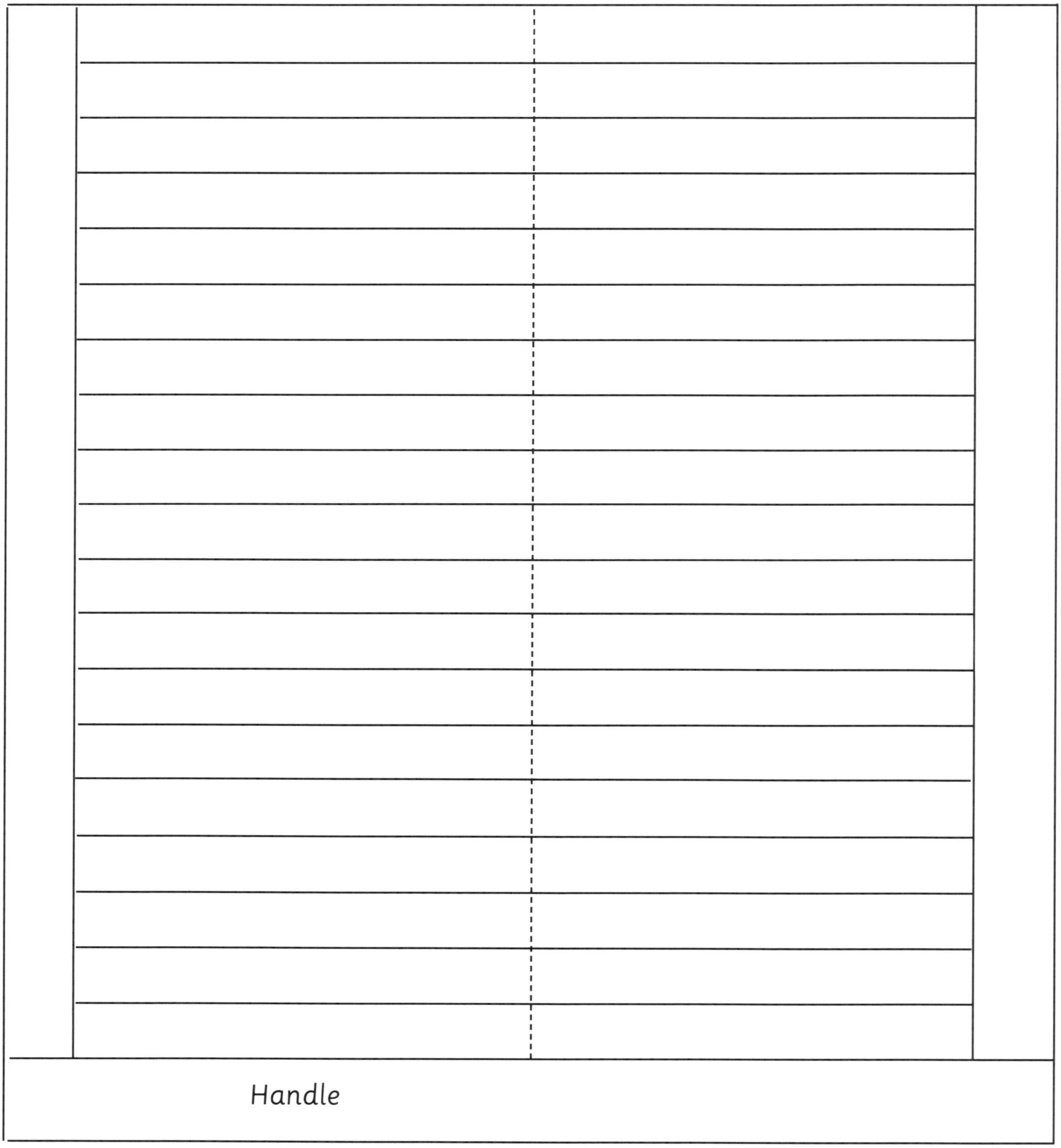

Paper Mat

1. Colour all the strips on both rectangle A and B.
2. Cut out rectangles A and B along the bold lines.
3. Fold rectangle A carefully in half from point x to point y.
4. Cut along the lines on the folded rectangle (make sure you don't cut right to the end of the paper).
5. Cut along the lines on rectangle B until you have sixteen separate strips.
6. Weave the separate strips into rectangle A (see diagram).
7. Put a little glue where the strips meet the end.

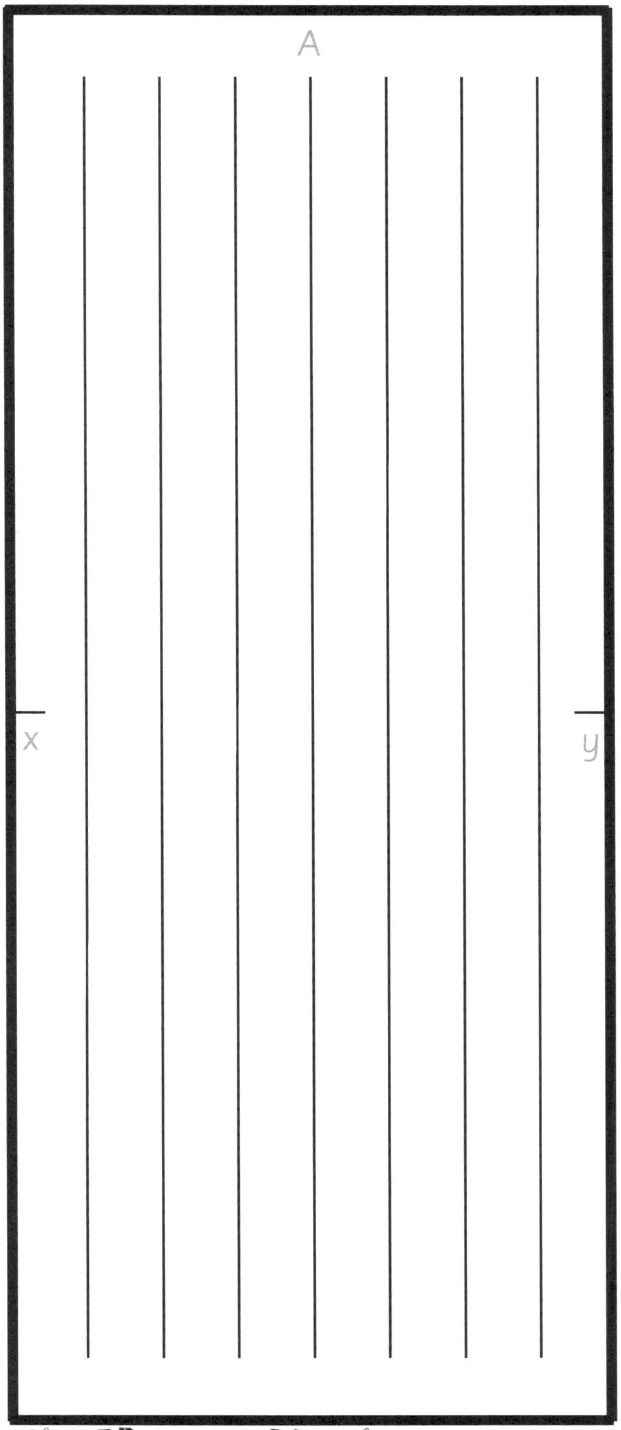

Make a Snake

tail

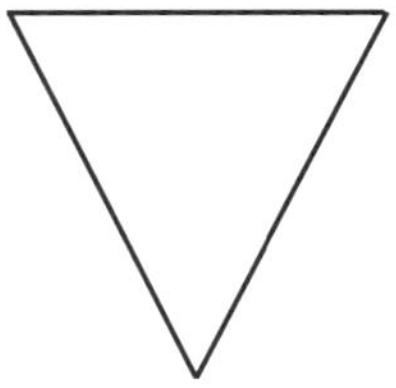

tongue

1. Colour the strips in different colours and patterns.
2. Cut them out and colour the reverse side of each strip.
3. Place one strip over the other as shown in diagram 1.

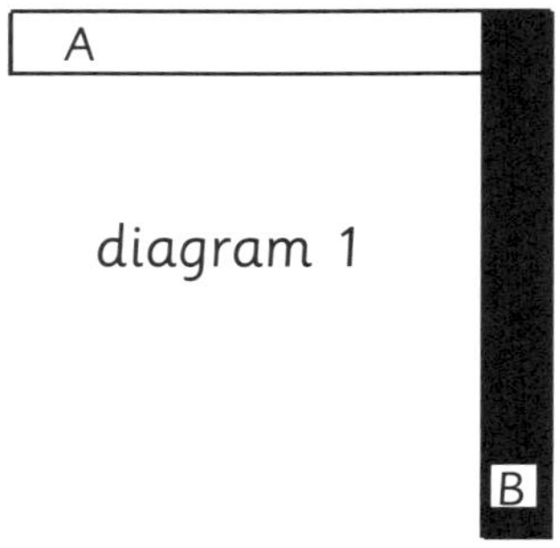

diagram 1

4. Fold strip B under Strip A so that it looks like diagram 2.

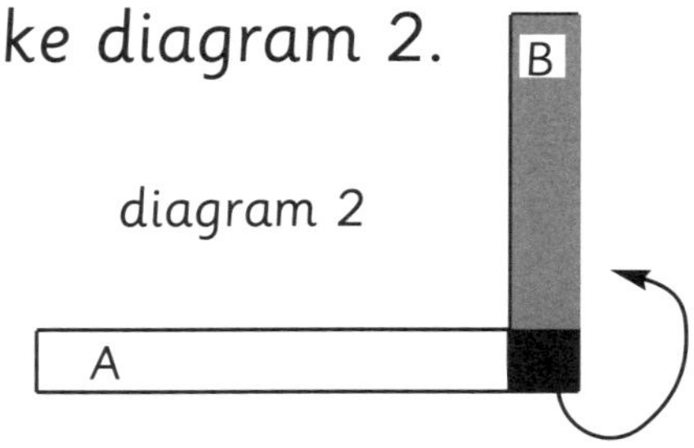

diagram 2

5. Fold strip A under strip B, see diagram 3.

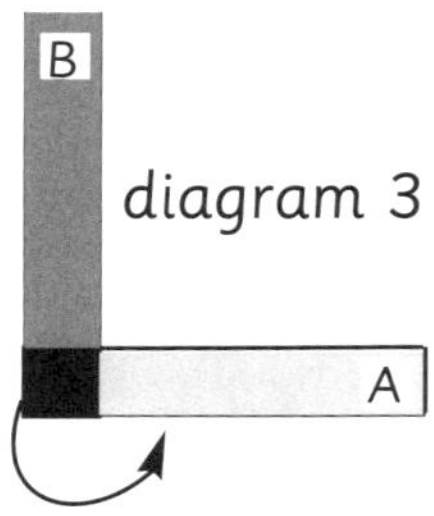

diagram 3

6. Continue folding each strip under first one way, then the other.
7. Glue or tape the top square to the square underneath it. Draw a snake's head on the top square.
8. Glue or tape the bottom square to the one above it.
9. Stretch the strip out.
10. Colour and cut out the tongue and tail.
11. Stick on the tongue and tail.

Coco Island

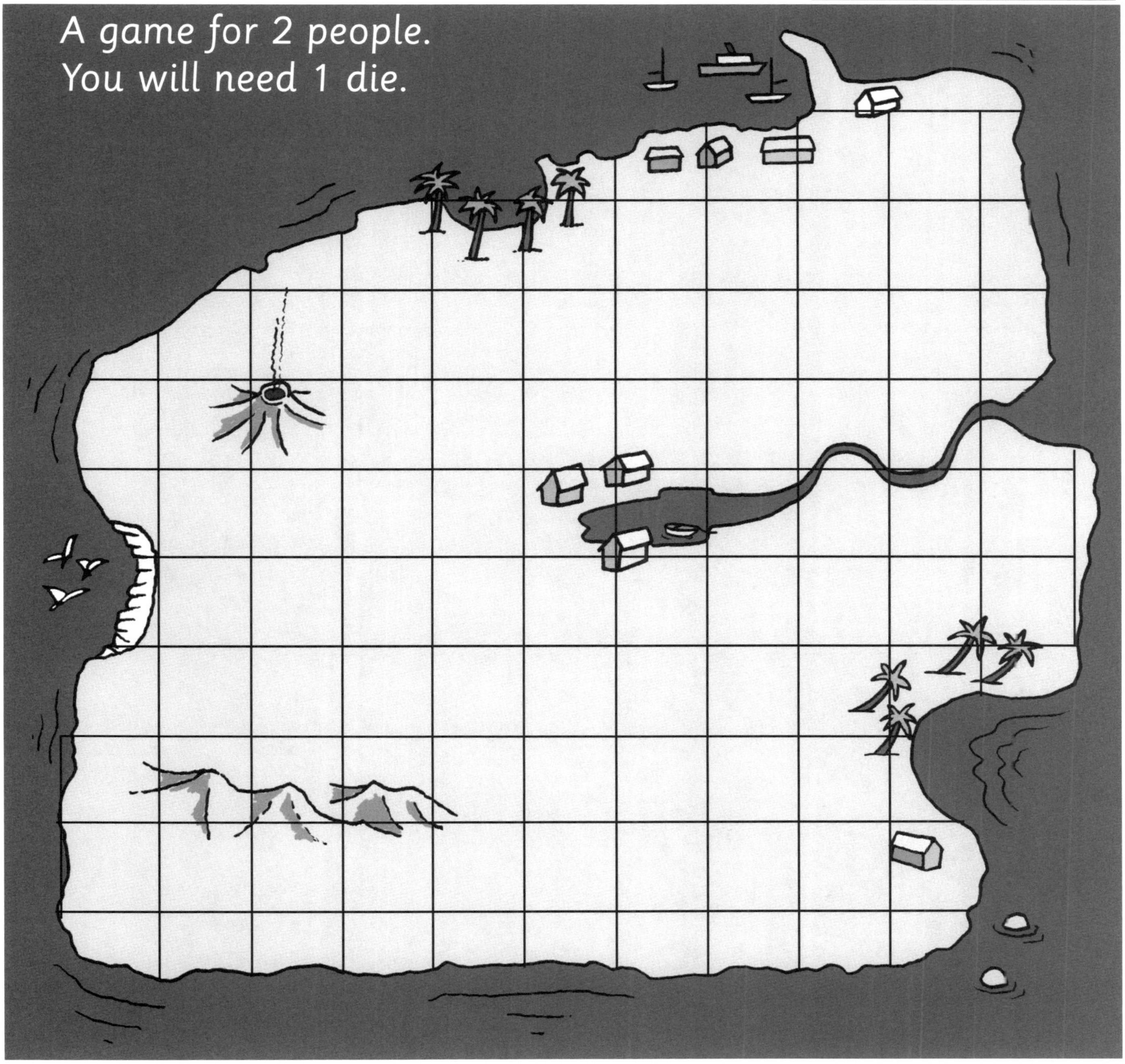

Who will win the most land on Coco Island?

✷ Decide who will be even numbers and who will be odd numbers.

✷ Take it in turns to throw the die. If you are odd numbers and you throw an odd number, then you can put your initials in any square on the island. You can then have another throw of the die putting your initials into squares as long as you throw an odd number. When you throw an even number you loose your turn and your partner takes over.

✷ If they throw an even number then they can put their initials into any square and continue until they throw an odd number.

✷ The winner is the player with their initials in most squares.

Airport Scene (1)

Use the grid co-ordinates to draw the picture of the airport.

3			
2			
1			
	A	B	C

Airport Scene (2)

Each small picture has a section of the airport scene on it.

C3

A2

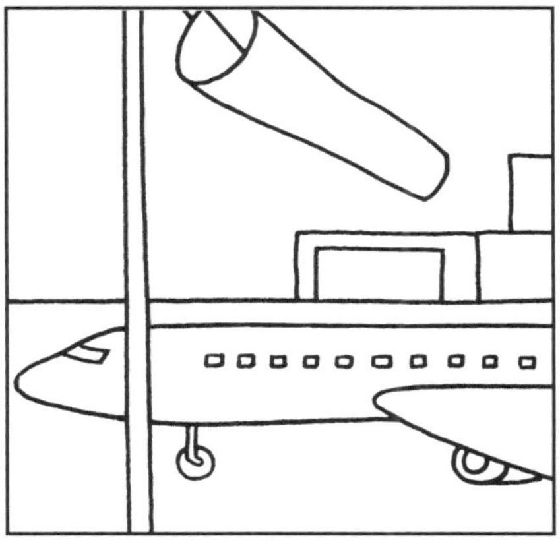

B1

C2

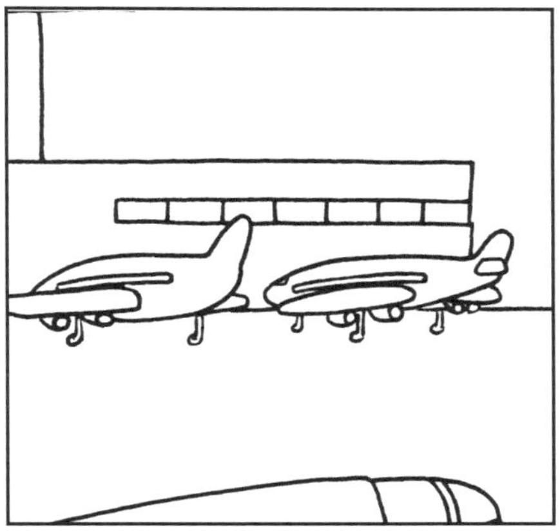

B3

C1

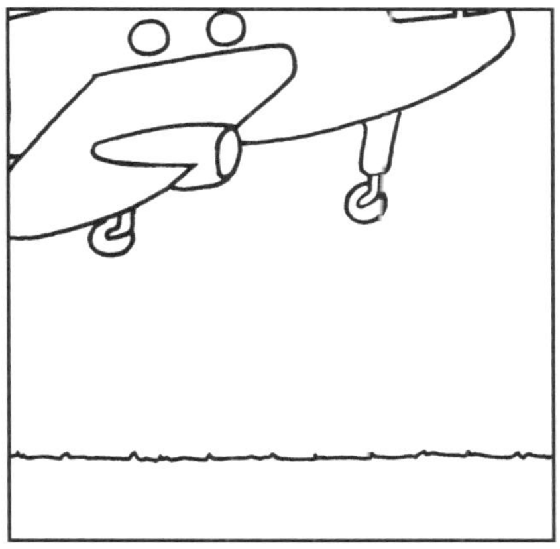

A1

A3

B2

Alien Invasion

An alien battle is raging on planet P743B. There are four different types of aliens. Can you work out how many there are of each type?

Number of aliens:

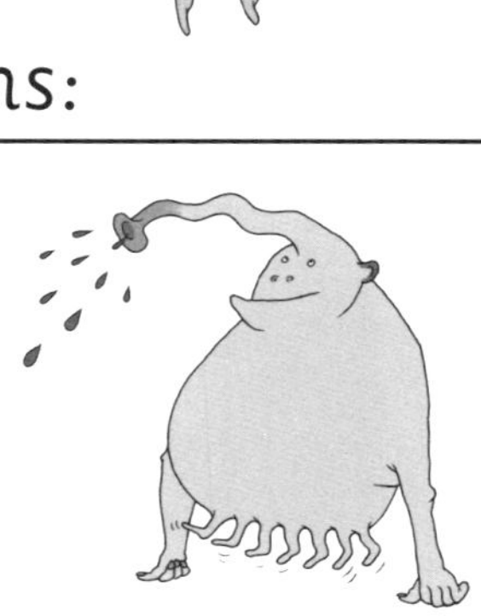

Memory Game

Play this game with a friend.
Look at all the pictures on this page for a few minutes. Let your friend hold the paper so that you can no longer see the pictures.
How many objects can you remember?
Your friend can put a coloured dot by each picture that you remember as you say them. Add up your score and then let your friend have a turn. Have several turns and see if you can improve your score.

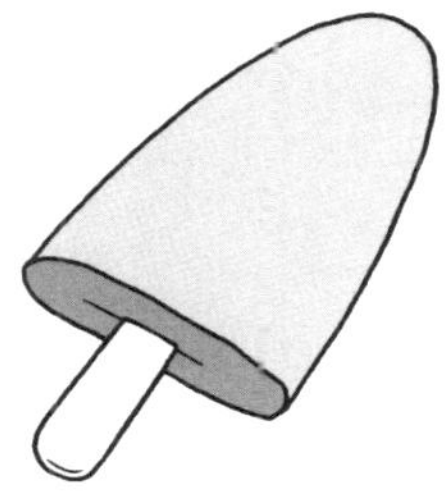

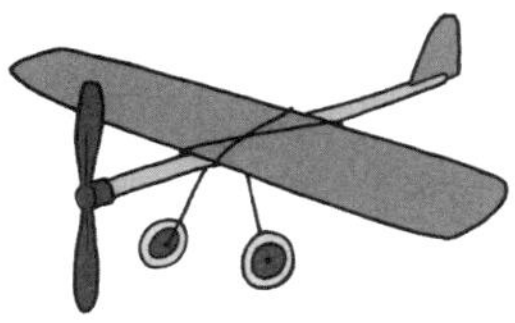

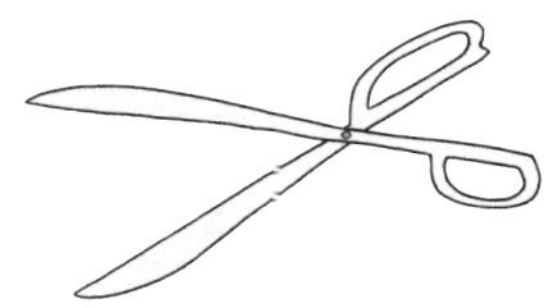
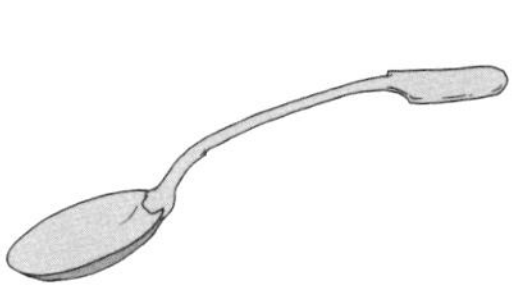

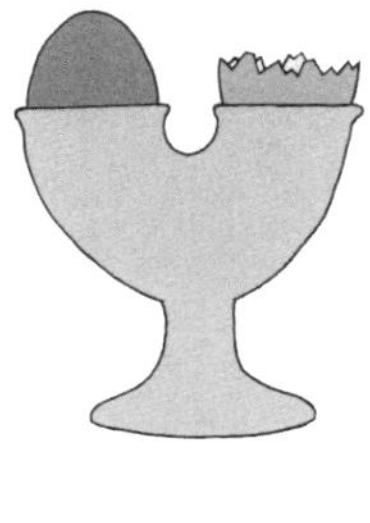
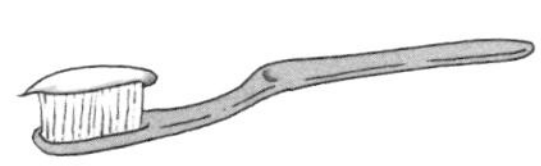

Lost Fruit

Which fruit appears the most times in this grid?

E	P	E	A	R	E	G	N	A	R	O	M
L	E	R	P	R	M	E	L	P	P	A	U
P	A	A	P	L	U	M	L	L	R	M	L
P	R	E	L	L	V	U	U	N	A	E	P
A	A	P	E	R	M	M	A	L	E	L	O
R	E	O	R	A	N	G	E	G	P	P	R
L	P	L	U	M	A	E	M	U	L	P	A
E	G	N	A	R	O	E	L	P	P	A	L
R	A	E	P	A	P	P	L	E	P	L	E

FRUIT	TALLY	TOTAL
PEAR		
APPLE		
PLUM		
ORANGE		

Put a line in the tally box every time you find a fruit and then count up the lines to get the total. Fruit names can be read forwards, backwards, vertically, horizontally and diagonally.

Suitcase Jumble

The labels on these suitcases have all got torn and muddled up. Can you put them back together again to make the names of eight places in the world? Some of the names have been torn into two pieces, some have been torn into three and one has been torn into four.

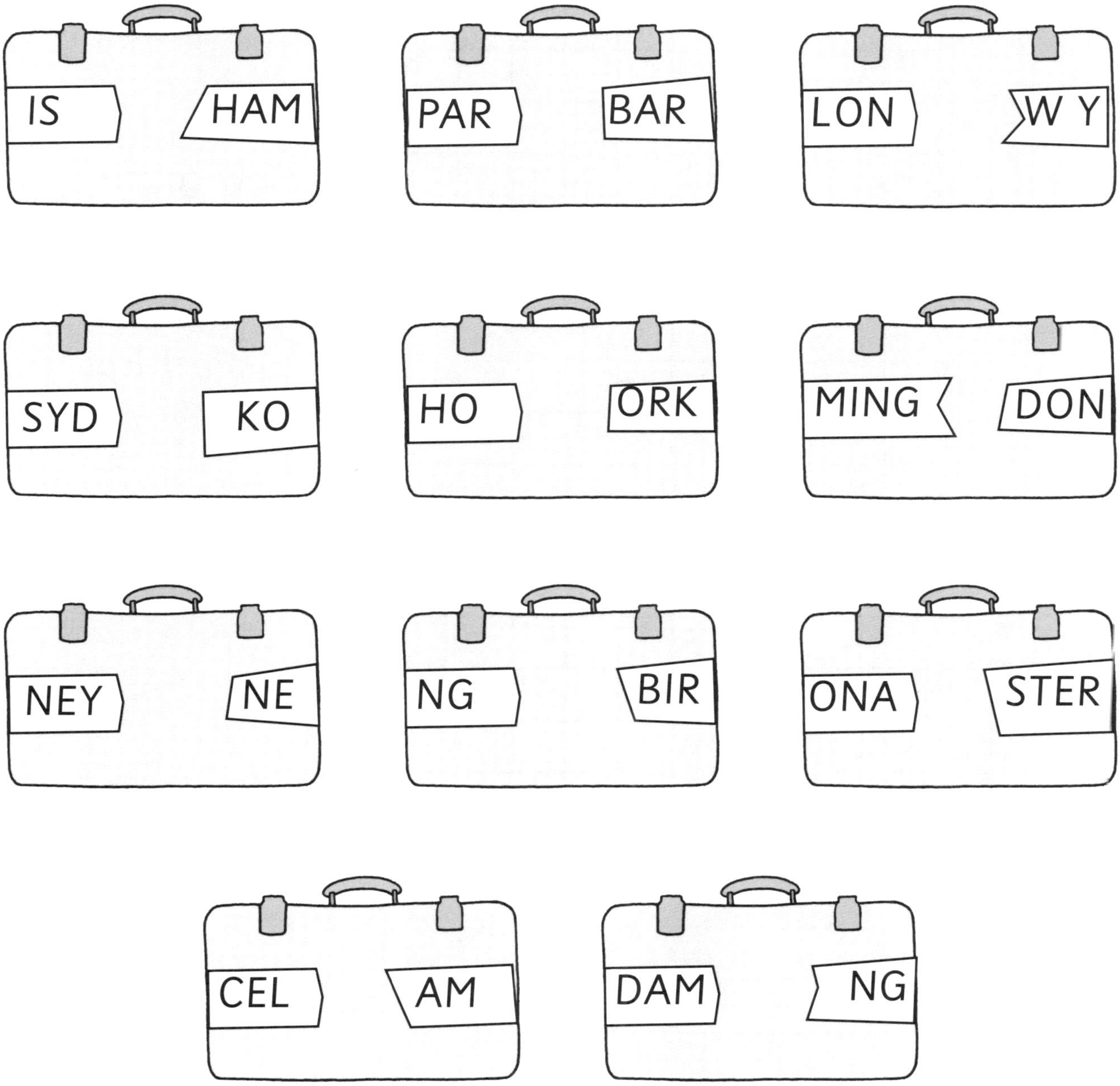

1 ______________________

2 ______________________

3 ______________________

4 ______________________

5 ______________________

6 ______________________

7 ______________________

8 ______________________

Symmetry (1)

Colour the squares:

R red B blue Y yellow G green

					R						
				B							
			Y								
		G									
	G										
B											
	R	R	Y	Y	G						
		G	G								
		B	B								
	R			R							
Y					Y						
	R			R							
		B	B								
		G	G								
			Y	R	R						
					B						
					B						
R	R	G	G	Y	Y						
G											
G		R	R	R	R						
B											
B	Y	G	R	B	Y						
					G						
					G						
				R							
			B								
		Y									
			B								
				R							
					G						

Now colour squares on this side, to make a symmetrical pattern.

Symmetry (2)

Use this grid to make your own symmetrical picture or pattern

Word Trains

Look at this word train:

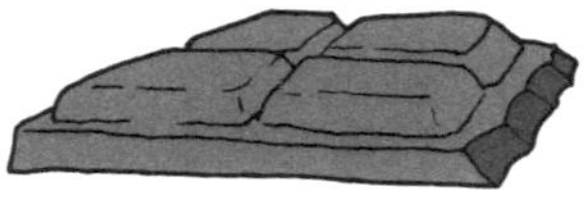

chocolate →

elephant →

tiger →

roof

forest ←

telephone ←

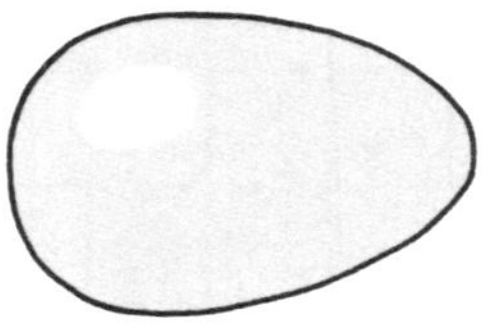

egg

glass →

sock →

kettle →

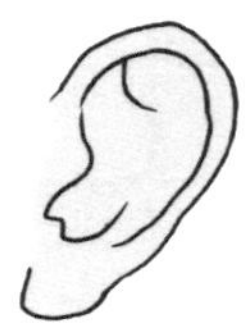

ear

Can you see how we made the word train? After the first word each new word starts with the last letter of the word before.
Try making your own word chain in the same way.
Draw pictures as you go.

Find Four

Aim - to make a line of four.

Equipment - die
counters in two colours
or two coloured pencils

Players take turns to roll the die.
For each roll one square corresponding to that number is covered.
If the number is not available then you miss your turn.
The first player to cover 4 squares in a horizontal, vertical or diagonal line is the winner.
In the case of the grid being full with neither player completing a line, the player with the most lines of 3 wins.

1	2	3	4	5	6
6	1	2	3	4	5
5	6	1	2	3	4
4	5	6	1	2	3
3	4	5	6	1	2
2	3	4	5	6	1

Hidden Trees (1)

In the writing below you will find ten tree names hidden. For each one you find, colour the tree name written on a leaf in the picture. When you have found all ten you could shade the remaining leaves a different colour.

I was lost and thoroughly soaked in the rain. I should have worn my helmet to save me from the water splashing down from the trees. One day perhaps I will own my own map - then I won't end up in this situation.

"I would like a map please," I had said when starting out, but there were none to spare. Then I got cross, had a row and stormed off.

I needed help earlier when I realised I was lost - but no-one was about. I really wished I had waited for my teacher Ryan and my pal Malcolm - they had a map! Never mind, I'm sure I will soon manage to find my way back and enjoy a nice juicy steak for supper.

Hidden Trees (2)

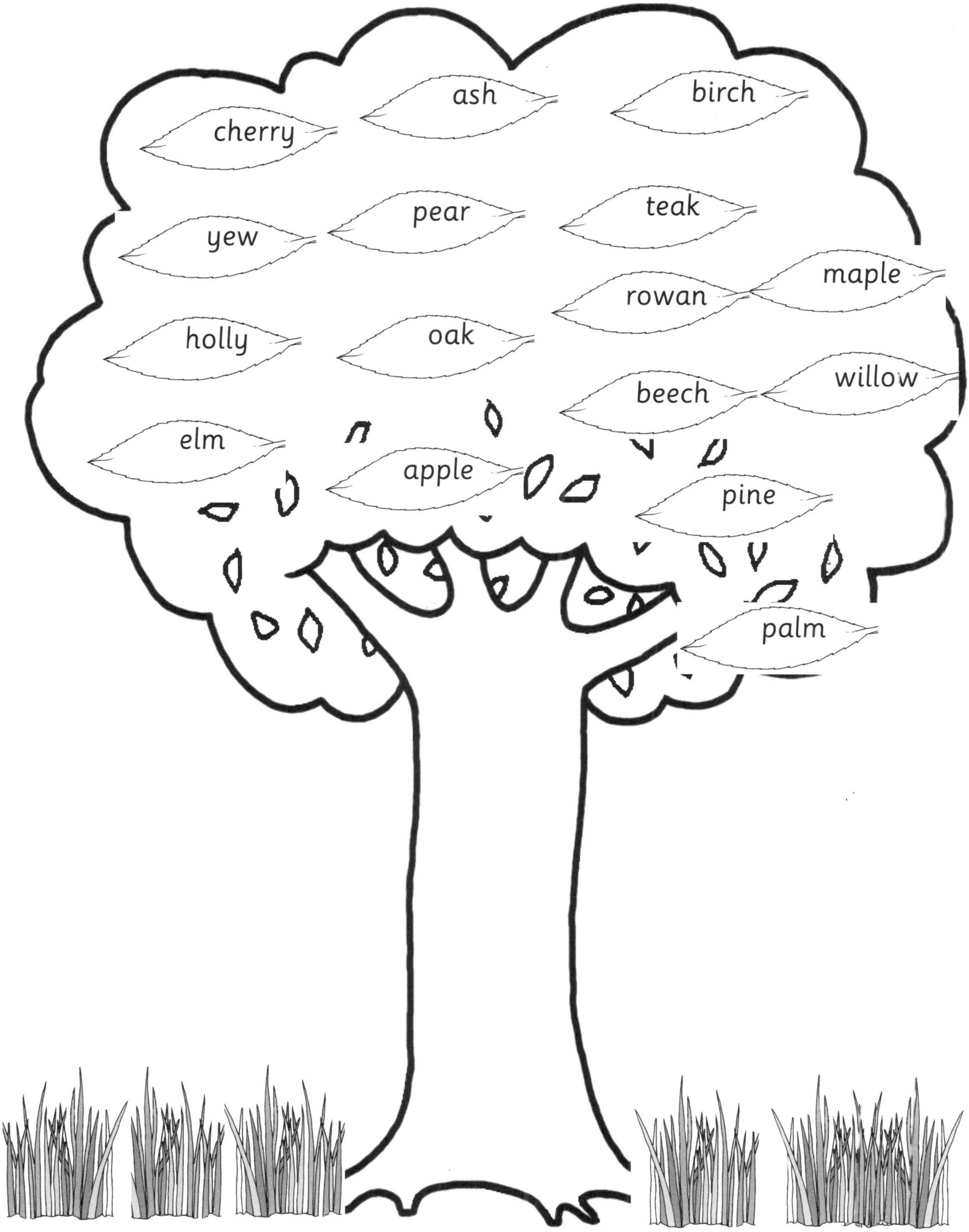

Word Games (1)

Take the word on the left and change the letters around.

Follow the clue to help you find the answer.

Word	Clue	Answer
bake	a bird has one of these	beak
pears	an extra one	
notes	a small hard rock	
rate	a rip	
lame	breakfast, dinner or tea	
pear	to harvest crops	
models	very rarely	
pale	a long jump	
earth	this pumps blood	
shore	animal to ride on	

Now try to make up 2 puzzles of your own

Word Games (2)

Put one more letter in each word to find the answer. The first one has been done for you.

Word	Clue	Answer
chef	person in charge	chief
old	precious metal	
log	a type of shoe	
hair	sit on this	
man	unkind	
heath	part of the fireplace	
hat	warmth	
pear	a sharp weapon	
hop	a place to buy things	
rip	a tight hold	

Now try to make up 2 puzzles of your own

Animal Madness (1)

Follow the clues to find the animals.

1. A type of large ape.
2. Dog-like animal, said to laugh.
3. Australian wild dog.
4. Related to a horse, sometimes found on beach.
5. Large spotted African cat.
6. Friesian, Jersey & Guernsey are all types of _ _ _.
7. Black and white striped horse.
8. This animal can be ridden.
9. A type of primate.
10. Small, furry, nocturnal, rodent pet.

If you answer correctly you will see the name of another large animal in the darker squares.

Animal Madness (2)

Follow the code to find fifteen creatures.

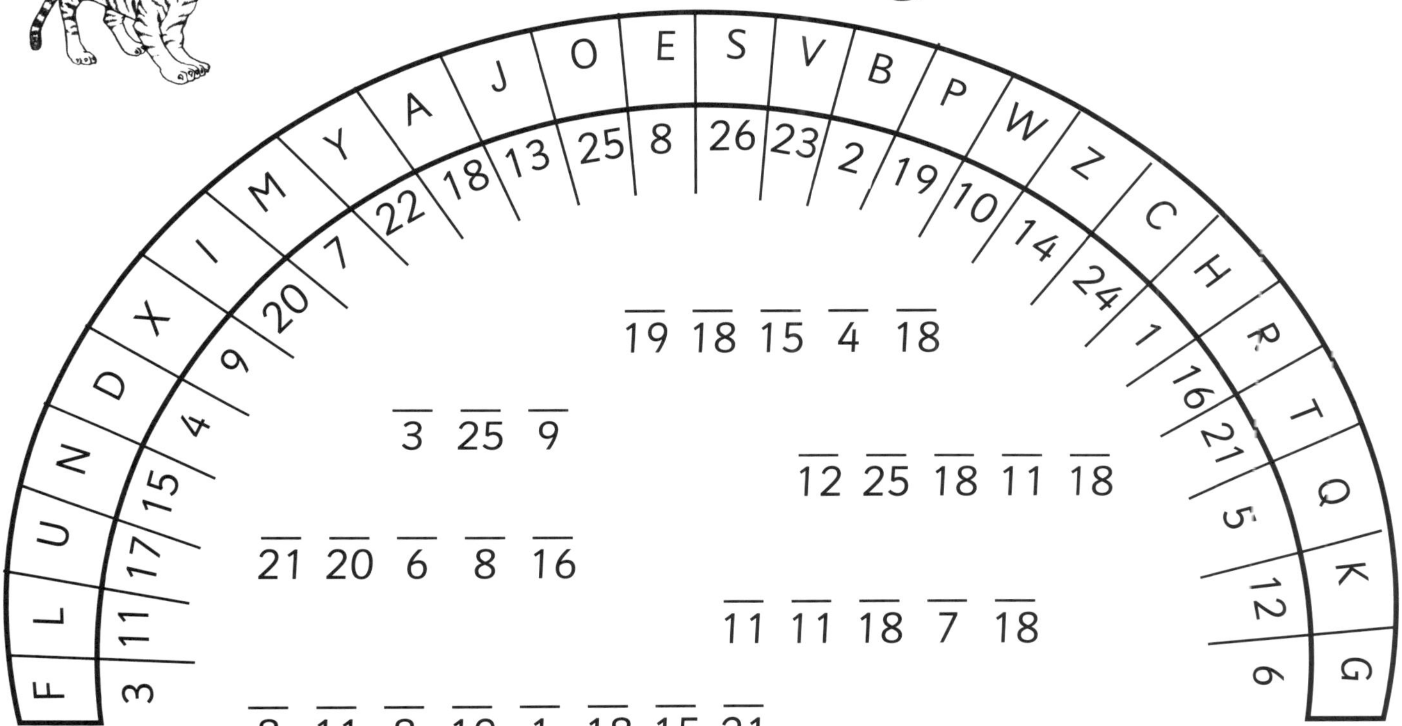

19 18 15 4 18

3 25 9

12 25 18 11 18

21 20 6 8 16

11 11 18 7 18

8 11 8 19 1 18 15 21

1 20 19 19 25 19 25 21 18 7 17 26

26 1 8 8 19

2 8 18 16

24 18 7 8 11

19 17 7 18

4 25 6

12 18 15 6 18 16 25 25

10 25 11 3

10 18 11 11 18 2 22

Watch the Birdie! (1)

The clues will give you types of bird.

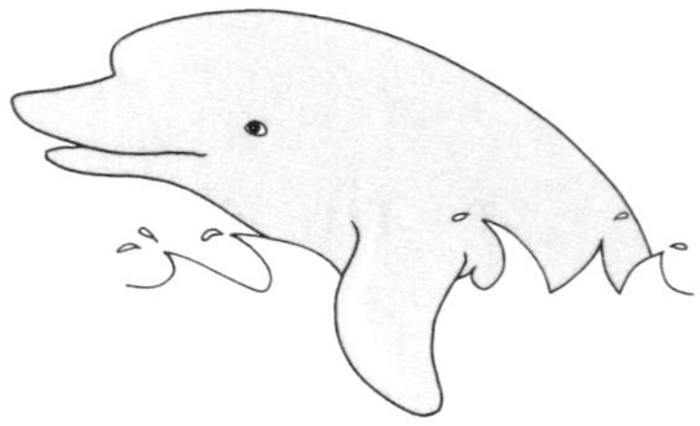

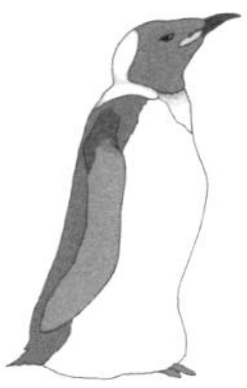

1. A common sea bird
2. A bird of prey, e.g. Peregrine _ _ _ _ _ _
3. Shortened word - a small bird often kept as a pet
4. Big bird of prey, sometimes golden
5. Bird sometimes eaten for Christmas dinner
6. Large glossy, black bird
7. Australian 'laughing' bird
8. White water bird with a long neck
9. Small common garden bird

When you have done them all, find the name of a large sea bird by reading the bold squares from top to bottom.

Watch the Birdie! (2)

Crack the code to find more birds.

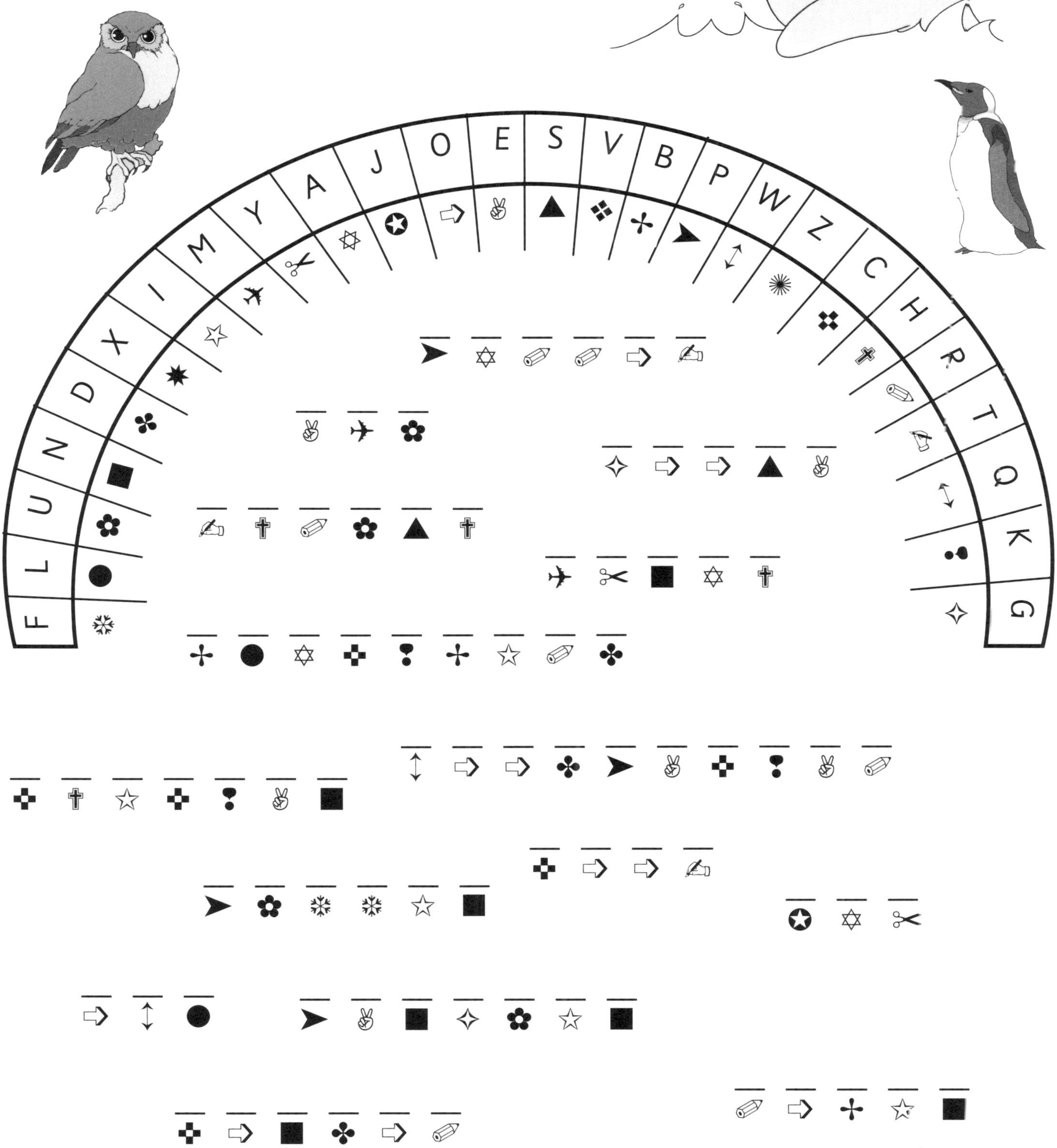

What a Tale

16 animals are hidden in the story, can you find them?

The first one has been done for you.

emu mouse lamb weasel

cow rat frog hare

cat dog ape pig

Chip Amberly and his mother Pearl were on the way to town in the family car. "I like music," said Chip, ignoring his mother's requests to turn down the volume. She scowled and continued driving along the road.
"Look!" shouted Chip in amazement. Further down the road was a mad ogre scattering brass nails across the street.
"Out of the way!" the pair yelled, but the deaf rogue continued trying to cause punctures.
"Whatever shall we do?" asked Pearl.
"Ha-ha," responded Chip. "Let's go left with the car at the next corner to avoid the nails."
After parking the car, the shopping was done. Amongst other things they bought a new easel, a pen, a box of enormous eggs and some fast oats for speedy porridge making.
"How can we get these eggs back safely?" asked Chip.
"Put the box carefully upon your lap to keep them steady on the way home," answered his mother. They soon reached home and parked the car outside their house; number 27 Bagshot Terrace.
"Well that was certainly an interesting trip," said Pearl Amberly to her son.

otter snail stoat pony

Find the Food

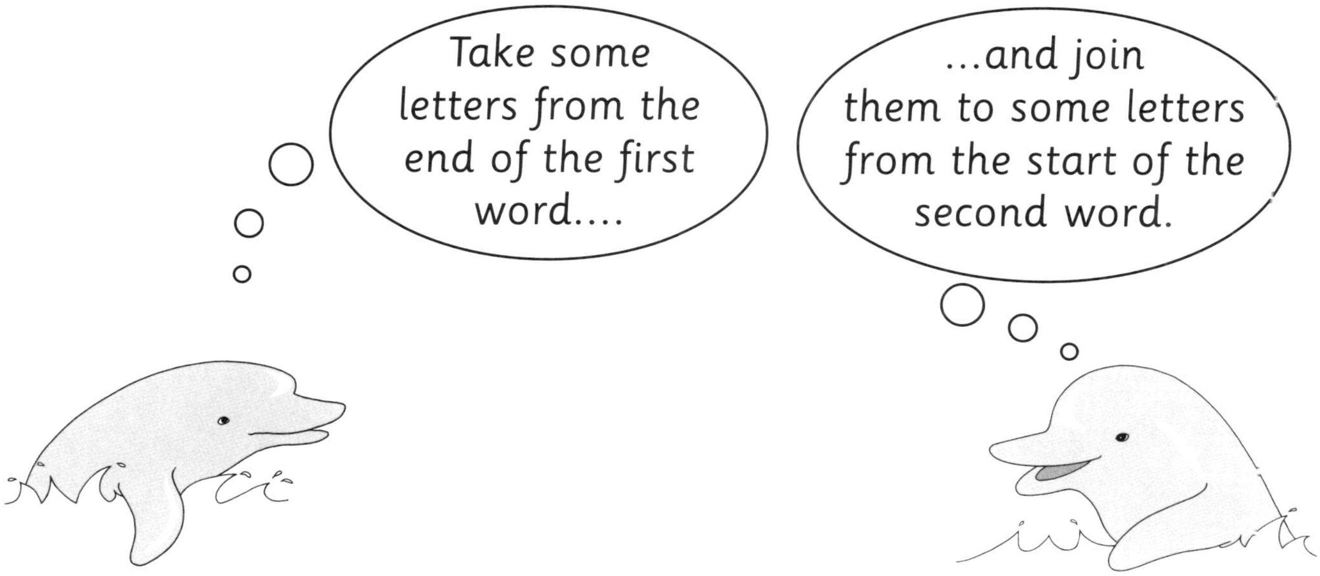

Look: PHOTO ASTONISHMENT

TO AST

Find the food in each pair of words:

CHURCH	IPSWICH	→ □□□□□
INCUR	RYEGRASS	→ □□□□□
REBUT	TERRIBLY	→ □□□□□□
PEG	GARMENTS	→ □□□
ALSO	UPSTAIRS	→ □□□□
WARDROBE	ANSWER	→ □□□□□
FOR	ANGER	→ □□□□□□
FEEDS	ALADDIN	→ □□□□□

Try to make up a food puzzle of your own.

Football

Riddle

Each line of the riddle below gives a clue to two letters. Choose the right one of those letters and you will spell the name of a football club.

solution

My first is in **action** and also in **stars.**

My next, not in **wage,** is in **transfer** and **cars.**

My third, not in **header,** is showing in **pass.**

My fourth is in **groundsmen,** but not **ground** or **grass**.

My fifth is in **shin**, not in **pads** nor in **kit**.

My sixth is in **match** and in **game** but not **fit.**

My last see in **whistle** but not **sing** or **hooters**.

My all has a name that reminds us of shooters.

The football club is ....

Try to make up a riddle of your own.

Football

Riddle

Each line of the riddle below gives a clue to two letters. Choose the right one of those letters and you will spell the name of a football club.

solution

My first is in **Beckham** and **soccer** and **score.**

My next is in **shout** and **chant,** never in **roar.**

My third is in **keeper** and **player**,not **ground.**

My fourth is in **league,** but not **team** and not **round**.

My fifth is in **offside** and also in **shoot**.

My sixth is in **trainer** and **laces** not **boot.**

My seventh is in **goal,** not in **lost** or in **won**.

My name you may think of when eating a bun.

The football club is ....

Try to make up a riddle of your own.

Football

Riddle

Each line of the riddle below gives a clue to two letters. Choose the right one of those letters and you will spell the name of a football club.

solution

My first is in **slide** but is never in **slip.**

My next is in **glove** but not **clothing** or **strip.**

My third is in **dive** and is also in **save.**

My fourth is in **cheer** but not **clap** or **wave**.

My fifth is in **tired**, and also in **fit**.

My sixth is in **goal** but not **leap** and not **hit.**

My last is in **stand** and in **fan** but not **queue**.

You'll find me in Liverpool, all dressed in blue.

The football club is ....

Try to make up a riddle of your own.

Football Riddle

Answers

My first is in **action** and also in **stars.**
My next, not in **wage,** is in **transfer** and **cars.**
My third, not in **header,** is showing in **pass.**
My fourth is in **groundsmen,** but not **ground** or **grass**.
My fifth is in **shin**, not in **pads** nor in **kit**.
My sixth is in **match** and in **game** but not **fit.**
My last see in **whistle** but not **sing** or **hooters**.
My all has a name that reminds us of shooters.

a	t
r	s
p	s
m	e
h	n
m	a
w	l

My first is in **Beckham** and **soccer** and **score.**
My next is in **shout** and **chant**, never in **roar**.
My third is in **keeper** and **player**, not **ground**.
My fourth is in **league** but not **team** and not **round**.
My fifth is in **offside** and also in **shoot**.
My sixth is in **trainer** and **laces** not **boot**.
My seventh is in **goal**, not in **lost** or in **won**.
My name you may think of when eating a bun.

e	c
h	t
p	e
l	g
o	s
a	e
g	a

My first is in **slide** but is never in **slip.**
My next is in **glove** but not **clothing** or **strip.**
My third is in **dive** and is also in **save.**
My fourth is in **cheer** but not **clap** or **wave**.
My fifth is in **tired** and also in **fit**.
My sixth is in **goal** but not **leap** and not **hit.**
My last is in **stand** and in **fan** but not **queue**.
You'll find me in Liverpool, all dressed in blue.

d	e
v	e
v	e
h	r
t	i
g	o
c	n

Colour the Sportsmen

Use these four colours to make the boys different: **Red** **Yellow** **Blue** **Green**

Colour each boy's clothes so that every boy is dressed differently.
For example, the first boy could have a red T-shirt and yellow shorts.
Each piece of clothing must have only one colour.

Colour the Sportswomen

Use these four colours to make the girls different: **Red** **Yellow** **Blue** **Green**

Colour each girl's clothes so that every girl is dressed differently.
For example, the first girl could have a red T-shirt and yellow skirt.
Each piece of clothing must have only one colour.

Follow the Pattern (1)

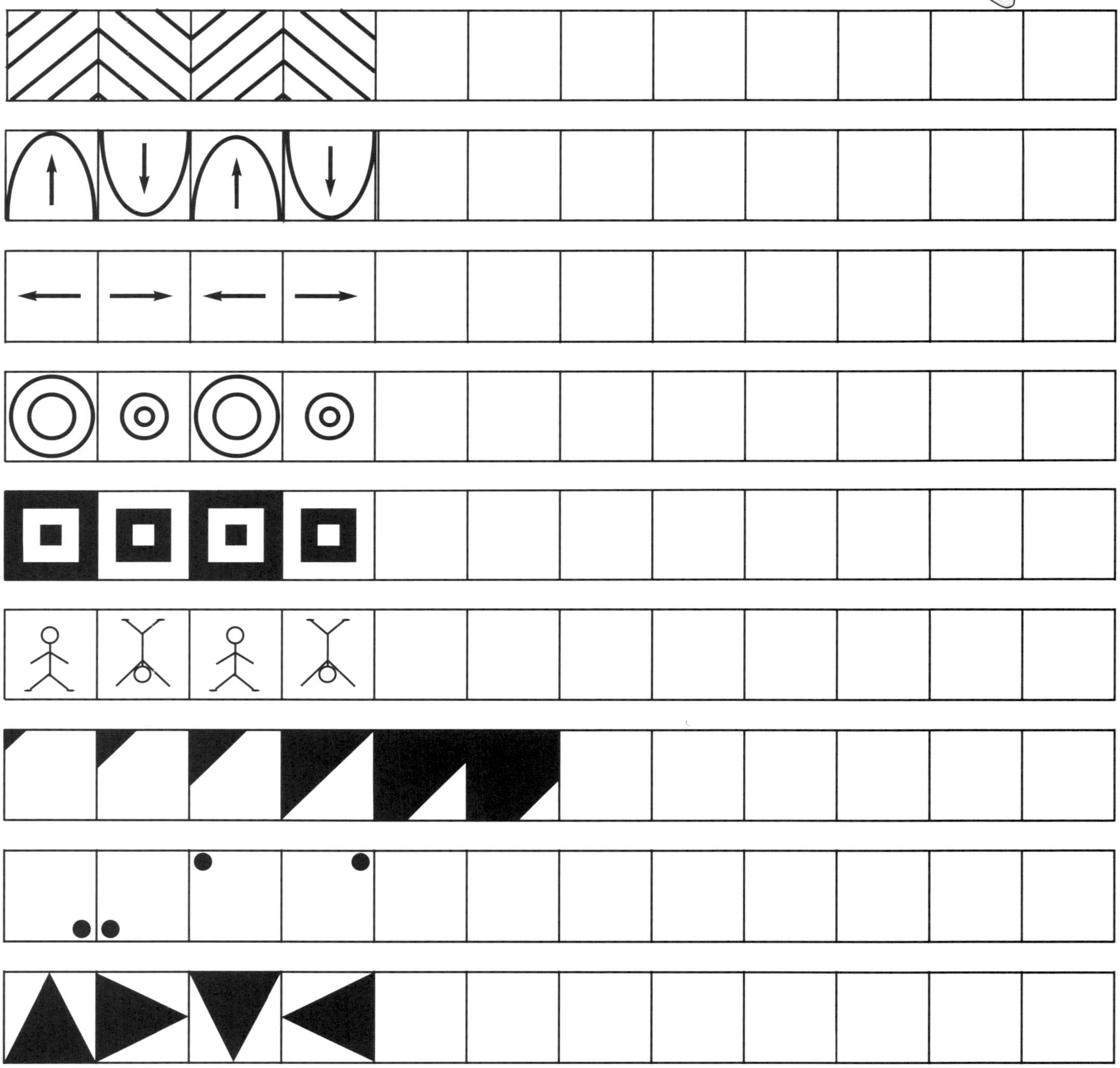

Try to make your own pattern:

Follow the Pattern (2)

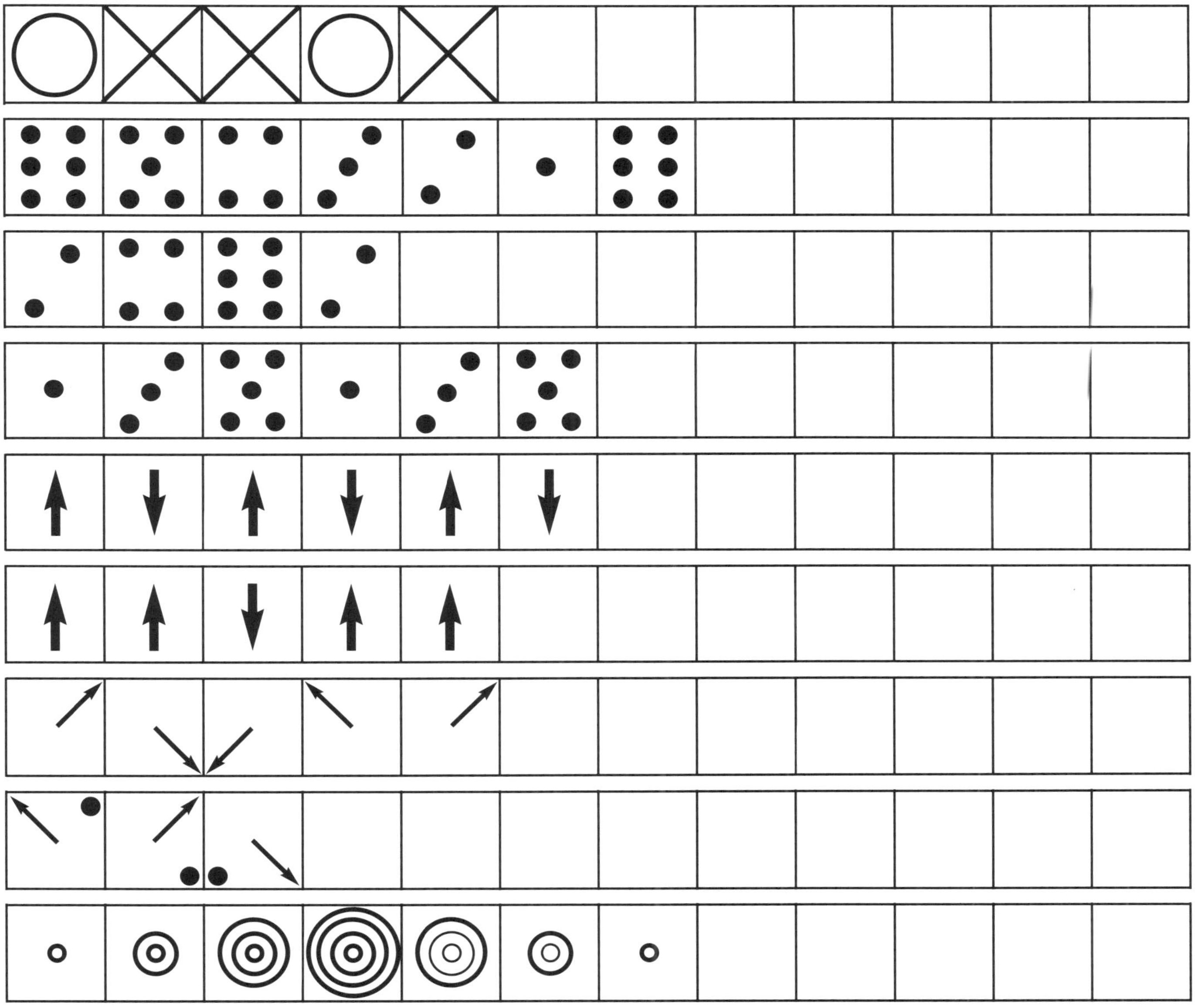

Try to make your own pattern:

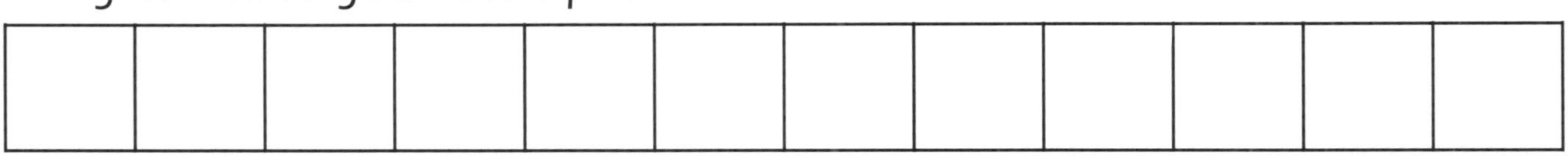

Follow the Path (1)

Follow the monkey's trail. Colour the squares on his path blue.
Follow the squirrel's path and colour the squares red.
Follow the crab's trail and colour the squares yellow.
Now follow the crocodile's trail and colour his route in green.

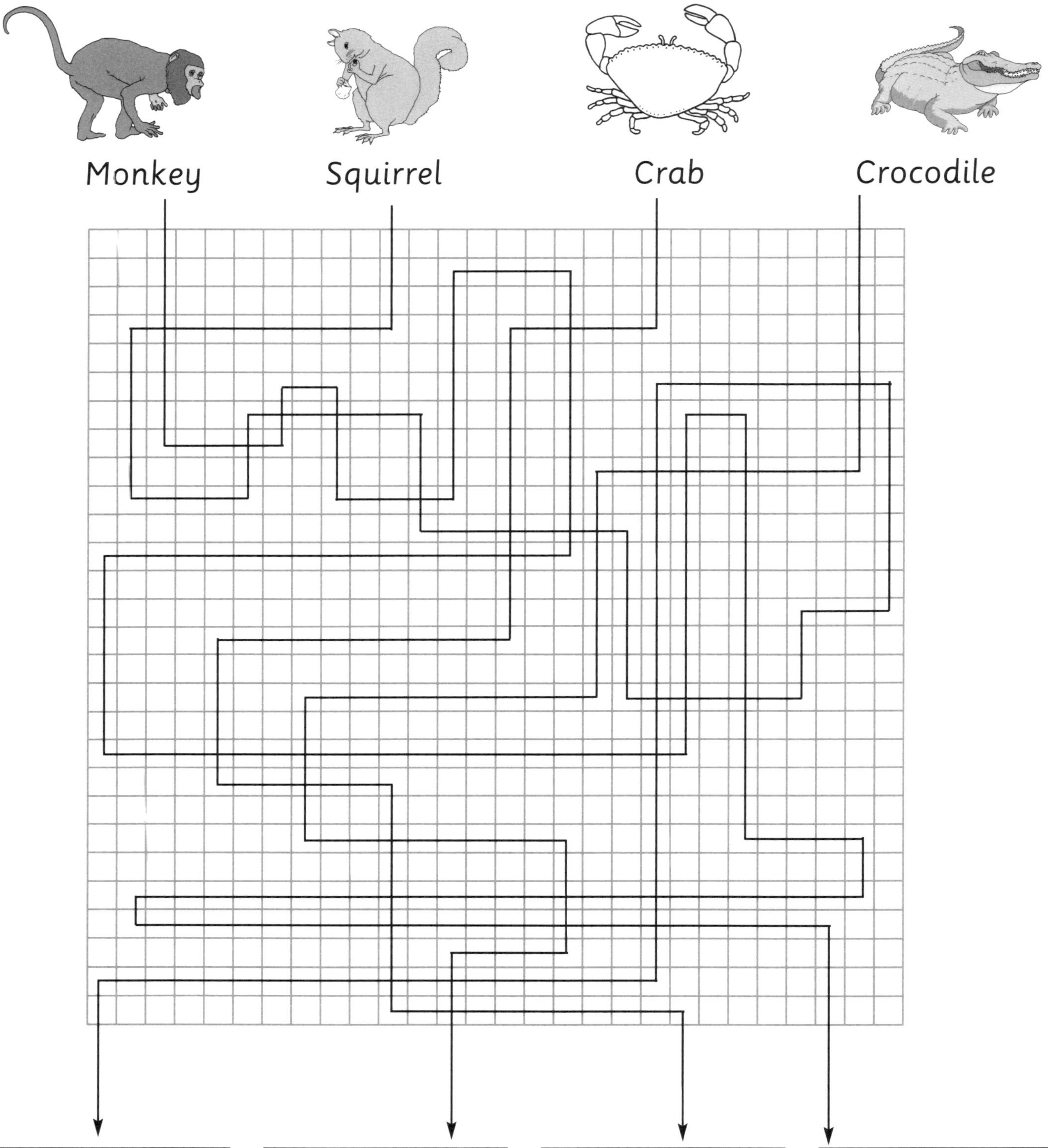

Write the names in the correct boxes.

Follow the Path (2)

Start at letter A.

Follow the path through the grid.

Write the letter A where the path comes out.

Now do the same for the other letters.

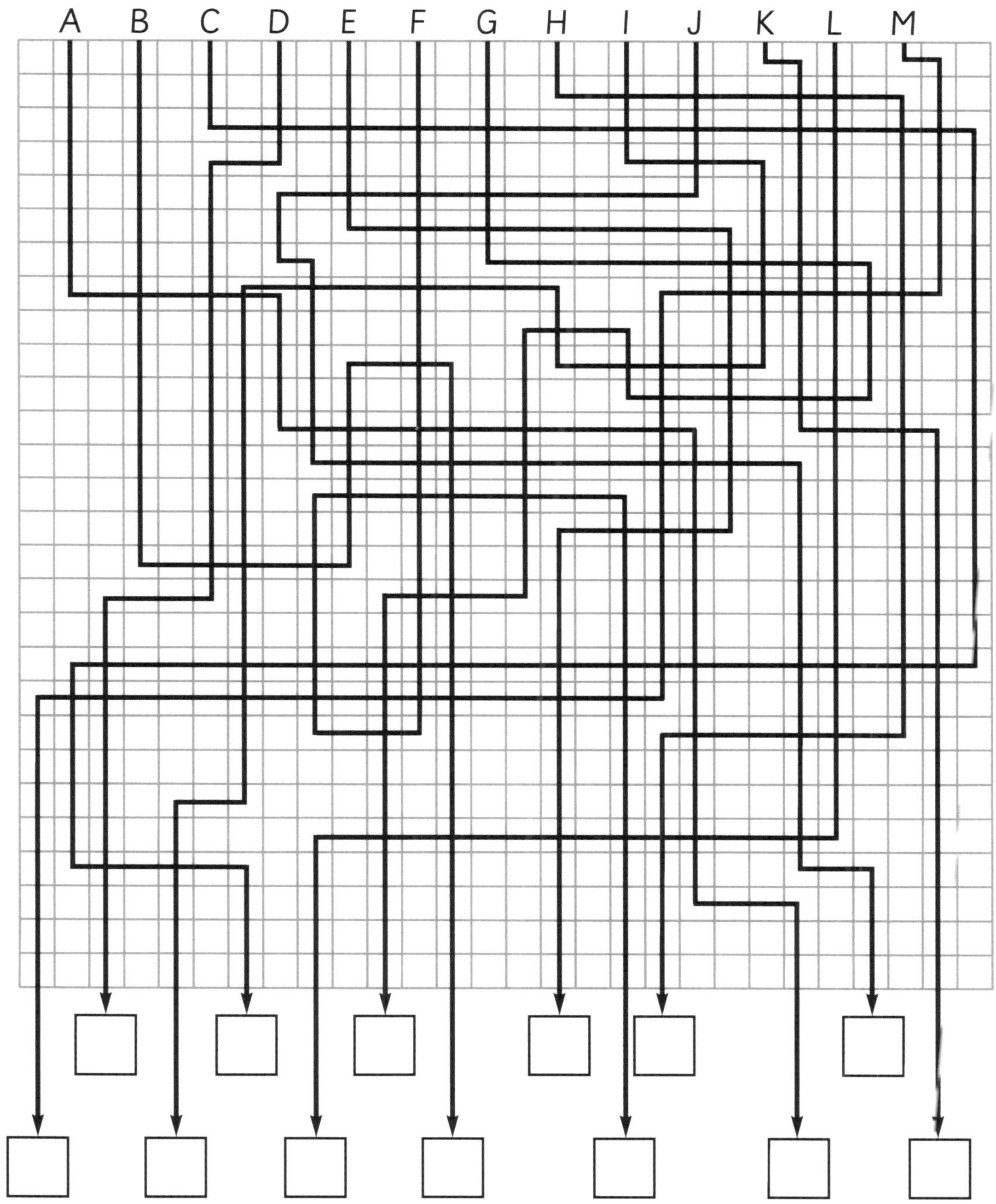

Where are the Letters? (1)

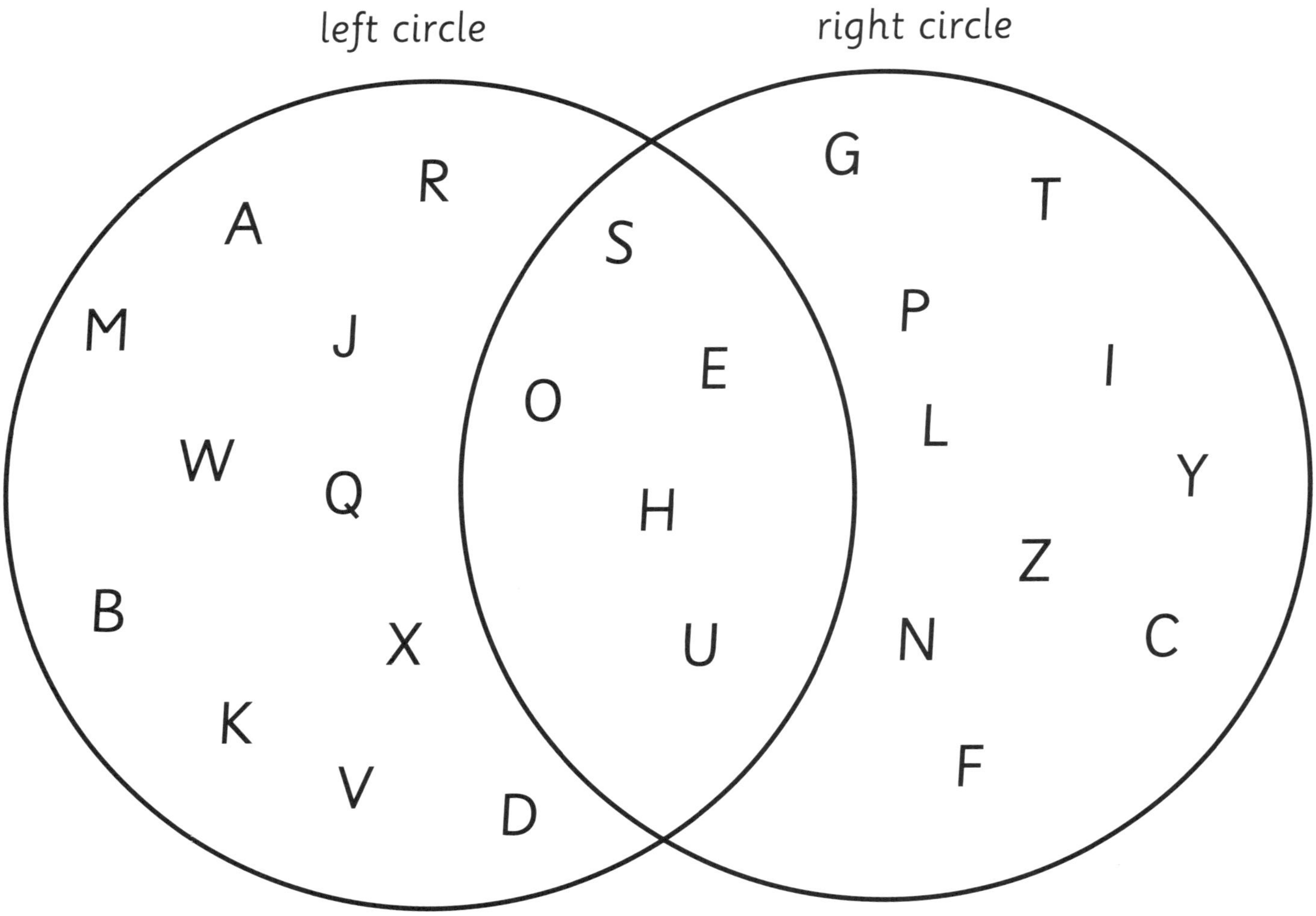

Which letters are in the right circle but <u>not</u> the left circle?

Which letters are in the left circle but <u>not</u> the right circle?

Which letters are in <u>both</u> circles?

Can you make three words out of these letters?

Where are the Letters? (2)

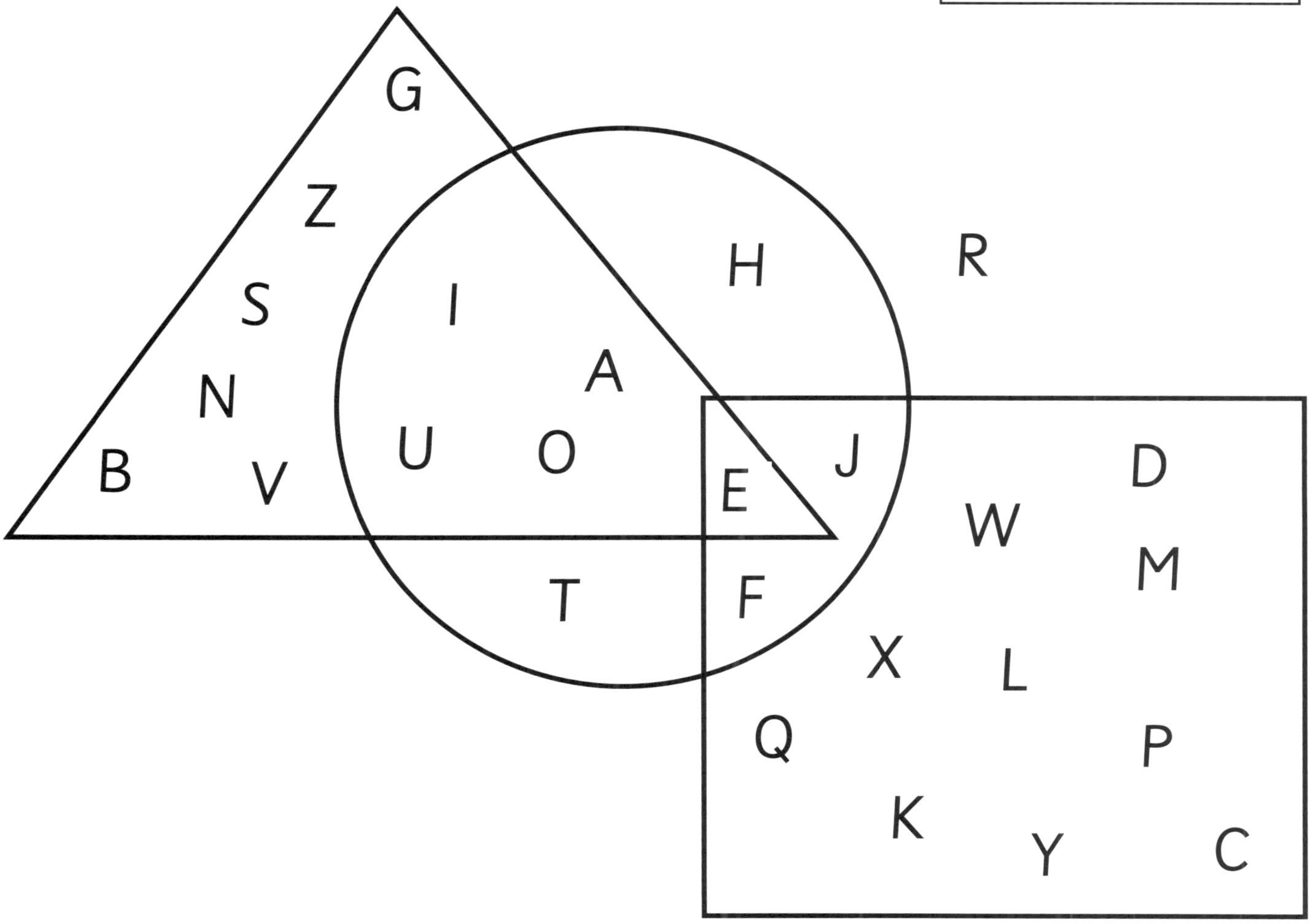

Which letters are inside the triangle?

Which letters are inside the circle?

Which letters are inside the square?

Which letter is not in any shape?

Joining Squares

Here are six different patterns made with three squares.

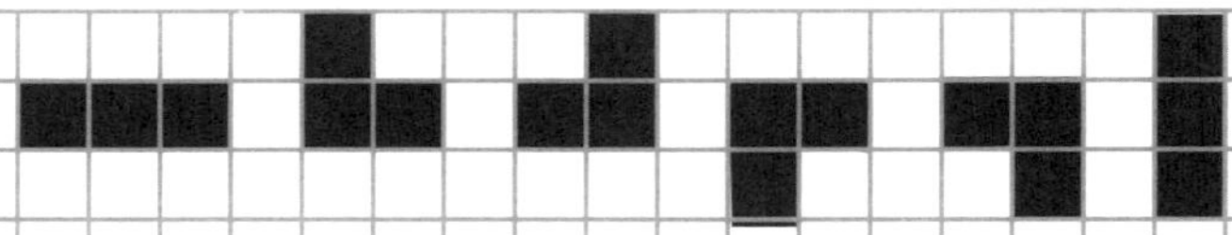

Here is an important rule:
The squares must join along a whole side.

They cannot join like this: 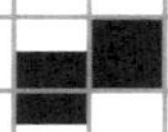 or this: 

Here is a pattern made with four squares: 

How many different patterns with four squares can you make?

Now try with five squares.

Design a Garden

I have just moved into a new house. Please help me plan a new garden to go with it.

Using whole squares and half squares design a garden plan.

- Between 60 and 110 squares must be grass.
- Between 10 and 50 squares must be flower beds.
- Up to 40 squares can be patio or paving.
- Up to 30 squares can be buildings such as sheds or greenhouses.
- Up to 20 squares can be other features such as ponds or trees.

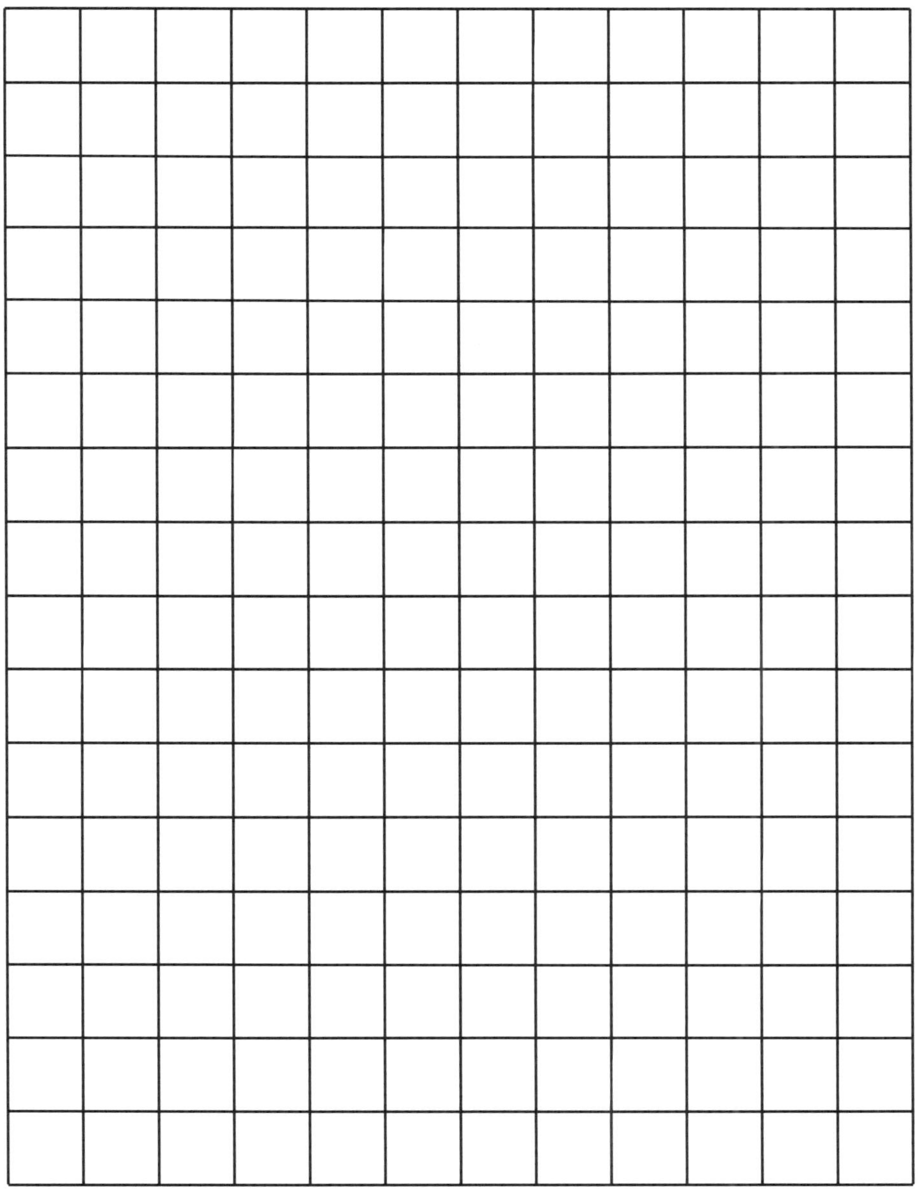

Make a coloured key to go with your plan.

Key

☐ = grass

☐ = flower beds

☐ = patio/paving

☐ = buildings

☐ = features

Walk Round the Island (1)

A word making game for 2 - 4 players.
(See separate sheet for instructions).

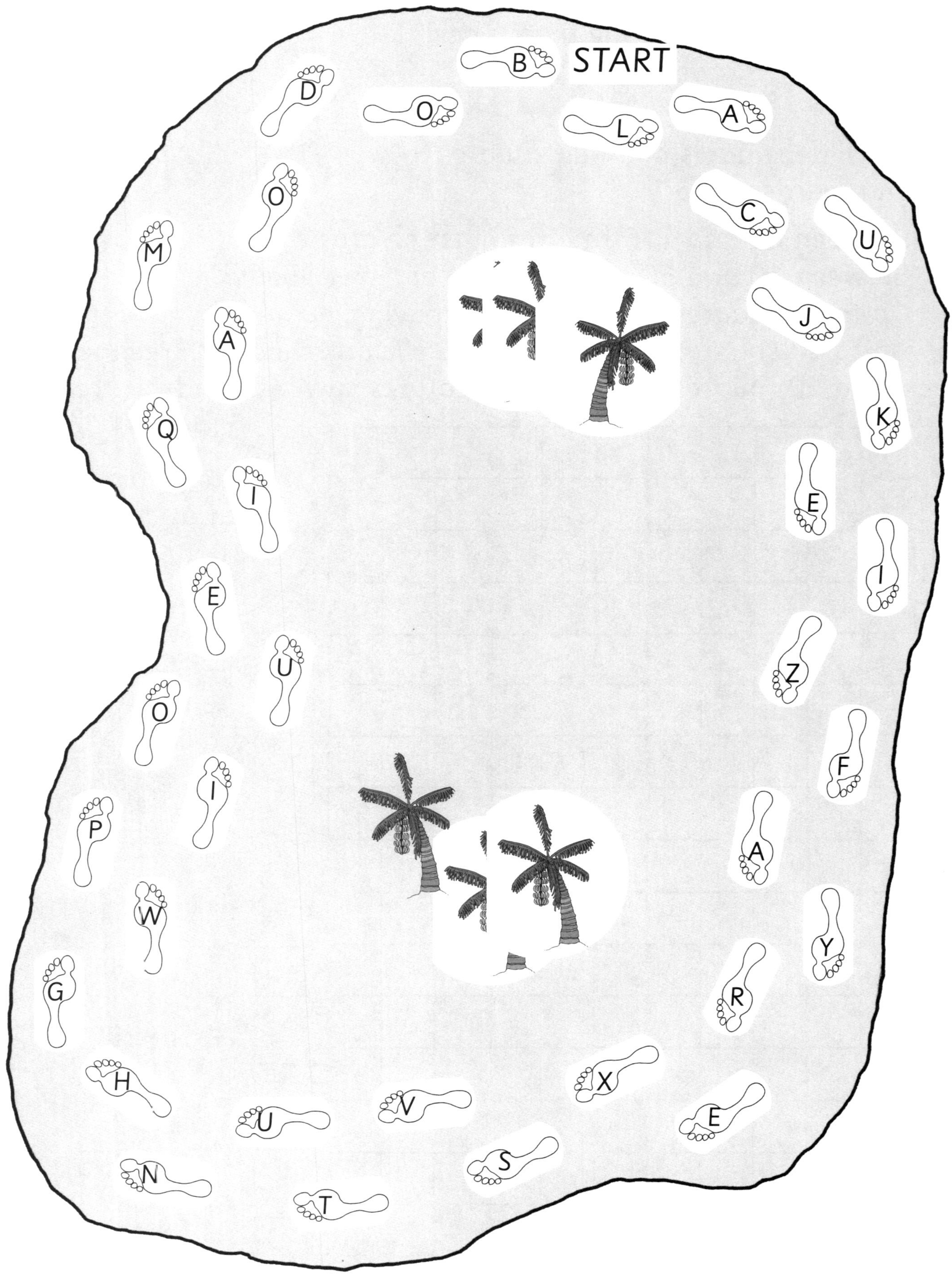

Walk Round the Island (2)

A game for 2 - 4 players.

Instructions

To play the game you will need:-

- 1 coloured counter per player (different colours)
- 1 game board
- 1 score sheet or piece of plain paper
- 2 dice marked 1 to 6

Aim of the game

To make the most words from letters collected whilst circling the island.

Method of play

- Players take it in turn to roll both dice and move around the island the total number shown.
- The player writes down the letter they finish the move on.
- Each player will have 8 turns, hence collecting eight letters.
- Players then make as many words of three or more letters as they can from their own letters.
- The winner is the player that makes most words.

Score Sheet

Player 1	Player 2	Player 3	Player 4

Word Square

- ❑ Make words of 3 letters or more.
- ❑ You must use letters in spaces joined by a side or a corner (so move horizontally, vertically or diagonally).
- ❑ You cannot use a letter space more than once in any word.
- ❑ Use a dictionary to check that your words are correct.

W	**E**	**T**	**P**
I	**S**	**F**	**L**
E	**N**	**U**	**A**
M	**I**	**T**	**Y**

You should be able to find at least twelve words here - you could find as many as twenty.
The first one has been found for you.

flat ________ ________

________ ________ ________

________ ________ ________

________ ________ ________

________ ________ ________

________ ________ ________

________ ________

Beginning in the top left-hand square (reading around in a clockwise direction), find a sentence and write it here.

Word Square - ANSWERS

- ❑ Make words of 3 letters or more.
- ❑ You must use letters in spaces joined by a side or a corner (so move horizontally, vertically or diagonally).
- ❑ You cannot use a letter space more than once in any word.
- ❑ Use a dictionary to check that your words are correct.

W	E	T	P
I	S	F	L
E	N	U	A
M	I	T	Y

You should be able to find at least twelve words here - you could find as many as twenty.
The first one has been found for you.

flat	**mine**	**few**
wet	**mint**	**sew**
play	**nut**	**west**
fun	**fat**	**win**
wise	**stew**	**nest**
use	**set**	**sent**

fuse **men**

Beginning in the top left-hand square (reading around in a clockwise direction), find a sentence and write it here. **Wet playtime is fun.**

Grid Picture

15											
14											
13											
12											
11											
10											
9											
8											
7											
6											
5											
4											
3											
2											
1											
	A	B	C	D	E	F	G	H	I	J	K

Colour these squares in blue:
D1
E1,E2,E3,E4,E5,E6,E7
F6,F7
G1,G2,G3,G4,G5,G6,G7
H1

Colour these squares in black:
E8,E14
F8,F14
G8,G14

Colour these squares in green:
A10,B10,C10,D10
E9,E10
F9,F10
G9,G10
H10,I10,J10,K10

Colour in these squares skin coloured:
E12,E13
F11,F12,F13
G12,G13

15											
14											
13											
12											
11											
10											
9											
8											
7											
6											
5											
4											
3											
2											
1											
	A	B	C	D	E	F	G	H	I	J	K

Boxes

A game for 2 players.

- Take it in turns to draw a line joining 2 dots. The dots must be next to each other either vertically or horizontally.
- The aim is to draw in a line that completes a box. Once you have done this, you may put your initial inside it and that is now your box. You can continue your turn by drawing another line. If this also completes a box then you put in your initials and continue. If you do not complete a box, then it is your partner's turn, who continues in the same way.
- When all the dots are joined, count up the number of boxes each of you has their initials in, to see who is the winner.

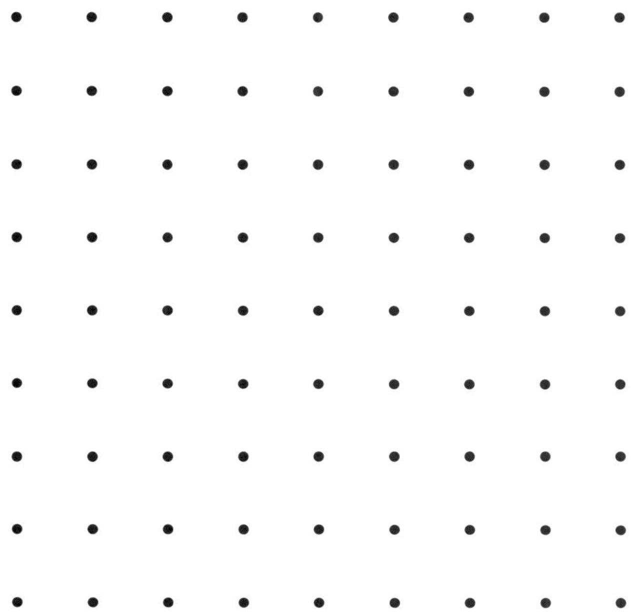

Triangles

- Colour one triangle.
- Then colour two triangles - they must be joined along one edge.
- Then colour three joined triangles.
- Then four joined triangles.
- Then five.
- Then six. Can you join six triangles to form a hexagon?
- How many different patterns can you make by joining six triangles?

Spirals

Here is a spiral pattern:
In the same way start a new spiral from the triangle that is marked with a dot.
Try to predict where the spiral will meet the edge of the grid.

Draw it

Draw the other half of these pictures as accurately as you can.

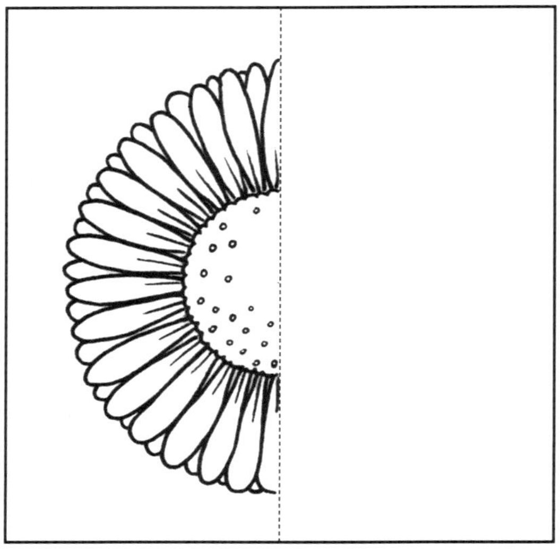

Draw one half of a picture and ask a friend to draw the other 'matching' half.

A Dice Game

1	2	3	4	5	6
7	8	9	10	11	12
13	14	15	16	17	18
19	20	21	22	23	24
25	26	27	28	29	30
31	32	33	34	35	36

For up to 4 players

You will need: 2 dice
3 counters of the same colour for each player

- Throw 2 dice and multiply the 2 numbers together.
- Put one of your counters on the square which shows the answer (e.g. if you throw a 4 and a 6 you will put your counter on 24 because 4 x 6 = 24).
- Take it in turns until each player has 3 counters on the board. It is possible for more than 1 counter to be on a square.
- Total up the number under each of your 3 counters.
- The winner is the one with the highest total. Use a calculator to check your addition.

Game with 100 Square (1)

1	2	3	4	5	6	7	8	9	10
11	12	13	14	15	16	17	18	19	20
21	22	23	24	25	26	27	28	29	30
31	32	33	34	35	36	37	38	39	40
41	42	43	44	45	46	47	48	49	50
51	52	53	54	55	56	57	58	59	60
61	62	63	64	65	66	67	68	69	70
71	72	73	74	75	76	77	78	79	80
81	82	83	84	85	86	87	88	89	90
91	92	93	94	95	96	97	98	99	100

You will need a die and a counter for each player:

Take it in turns to throw a die.
Move your counter on 1 if you throw an odd number, or 10 if you throw an even number.
The first one to reach 100, or the one on the highest number at the end of break, is the winner.

Game with 100 Square (2)

1	2	3	4	5	6	7	8	9	10
11	12	13	14	15	16	17	18	19	20
21	22	23	24	25	26	27	28	29	30
31	32	33	34	35	36	37	38	39	40
41	42	43	44	45	46	47	48	49	50
51	52	53	54	55	56	57	58	59	60
61	62	63	64	65	66	67	68	69	70
71	72	73	74	75	76	77	78	79	80
81	82	83	84	85	86	87	88	89	90
91	92	93	94	95	96	97	98	99	100

You will need a die and a counter for each player:

Take it in turns to throw a die.
Multiply the number on the die by 3 and move that number of spaces.
The first one to 100 is the winner. (You do not have to land on 100 exactly.)

Crossing the Page (1)

Start on the left side of the page.
Your aim is to cross to the right.
You can move 1 centimetre at a time.
The quickest way across is to go in a straight line. The slowest way would be to take a complicated route, sometimes moving up or down and even going in the wrong direction.
Look at Arnold the Ant's route.

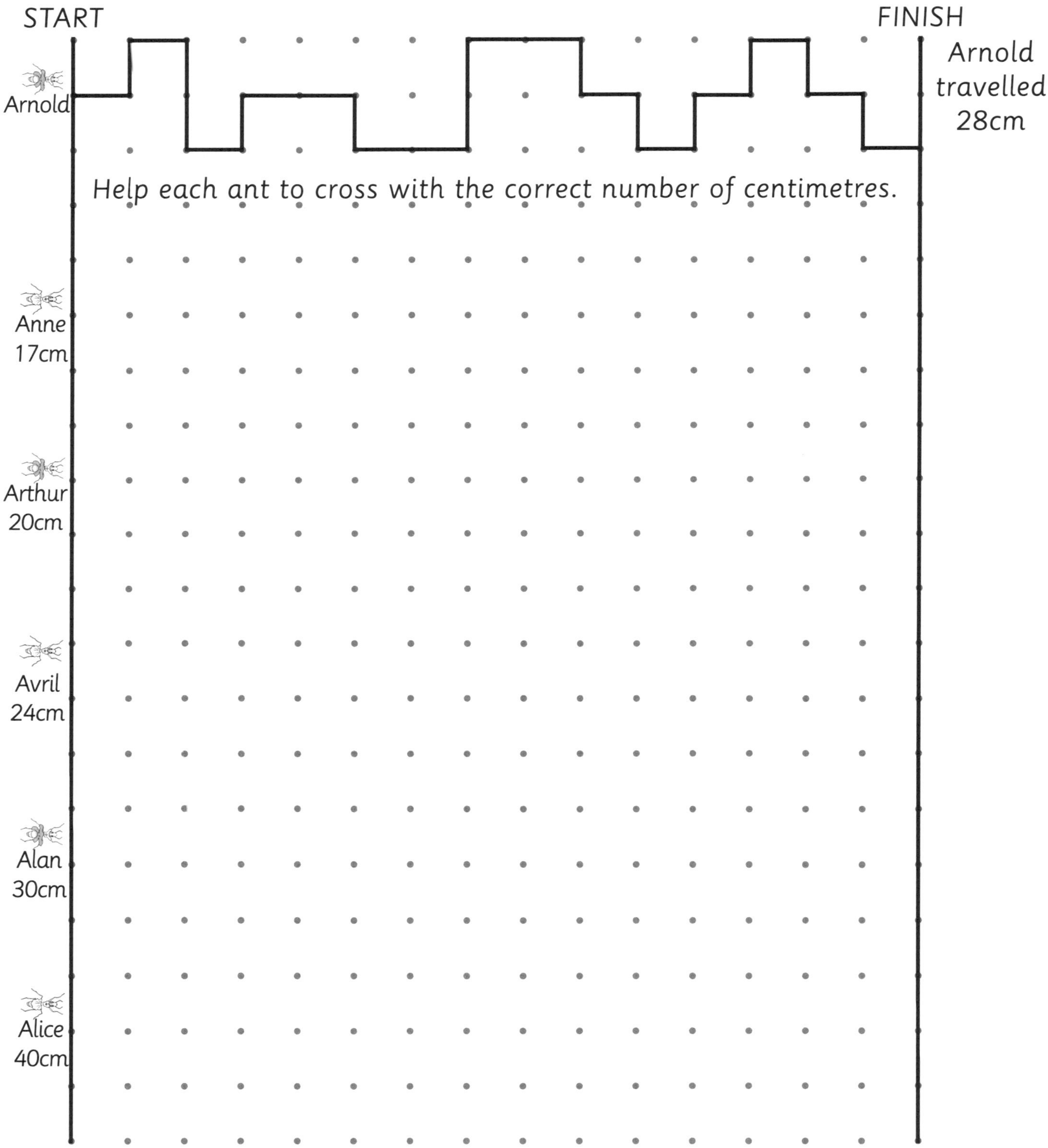

Crossing the Page (2)

Start on the left side of the page.
Your aim is to cross to the right.
You can move 1 centimetre at a time.
The quickest way across is to go in a straight line. The slowest way would be to take a complicated route, sometimes moving up or down and even going in the wrong direction.

How far would Alex the Ant travel if he went by the shortest route?

Help Abby the Ant to travel the longest route possible. How many centimetres does she travel?

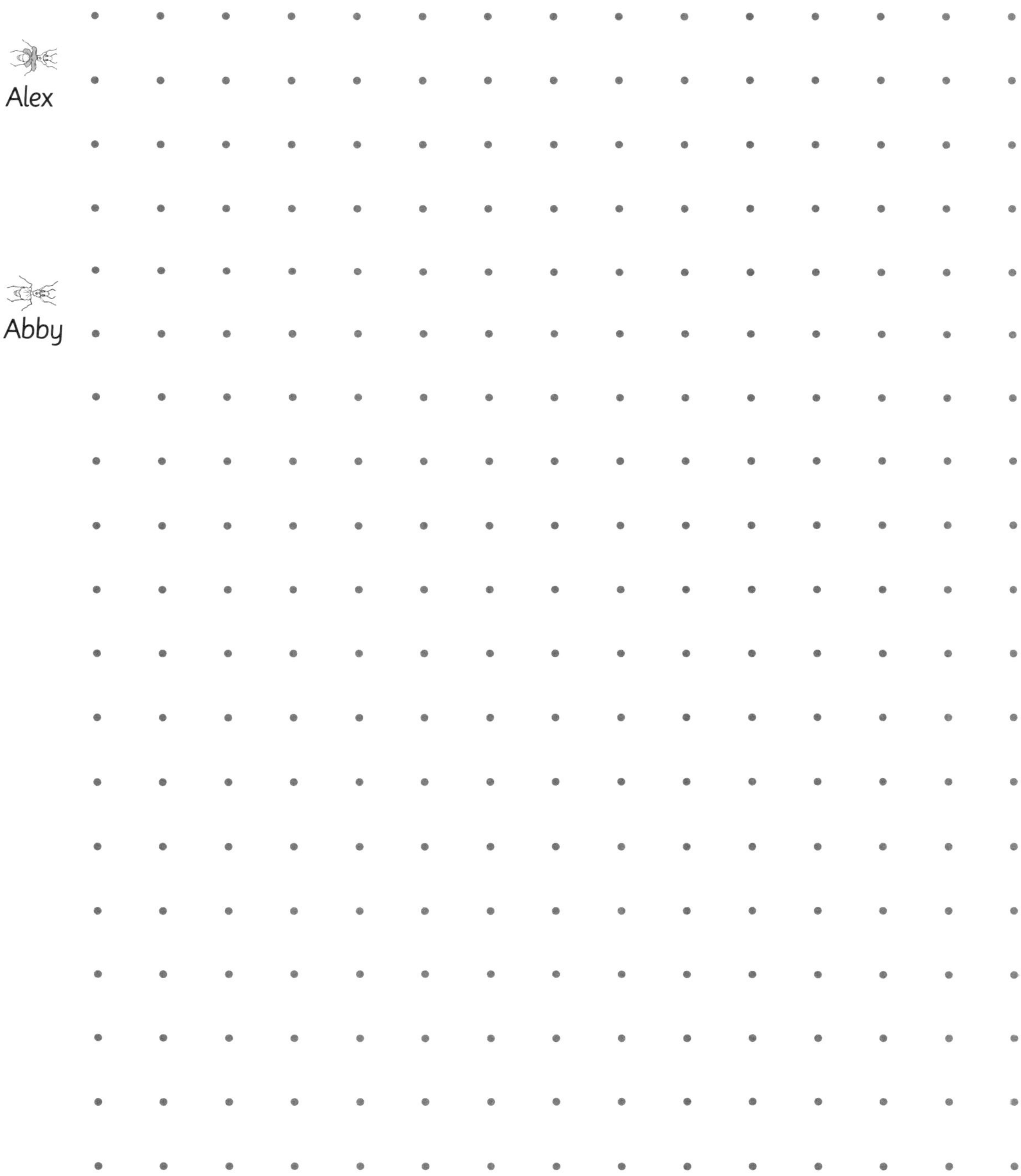

Alex travelled ....cm

Abby travelled .... cm

Crossing the Page (3)

Start on the left side of the page.
Your aim is to cross to the right.
You can move 1 centimetre at a time.
The quickest way across is a straight line. The slowest way would be to take a complicated route, sometimes moving diagonally up or down and even going in the wrong direction.

How far does Annette the Ant travel?

Annette

Annette travels cm

Help the other ants to cross using the correct number of centimetres.

Albert 30cm

Amy 26cm

Alex 32cm

Angela 40cm

Crossing the Page (4)

Rules of the Game

Cross the page by colouring triangles.

You must colour adjacent triangles.

They must touch along one edge like this:

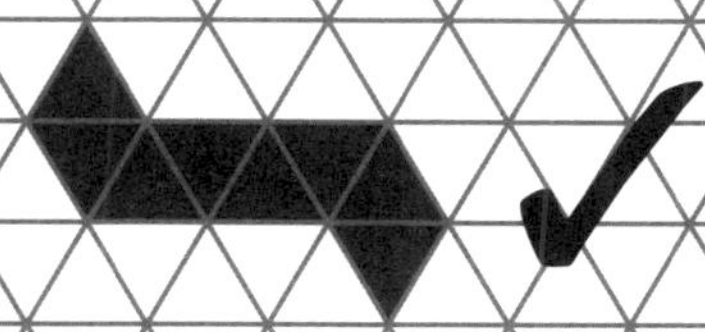

They must not touch just by their corners.

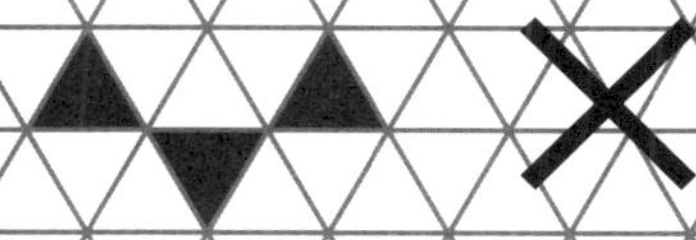

How many triangles do you colour if you go the shortest way?

Try to find the longest way across. How many triangles do you colour?

Crossing the Page (5)

Rules of the Game

Cross the page by colouring squares.

You must colour adjacent squares.

They must touch along one edge like these:

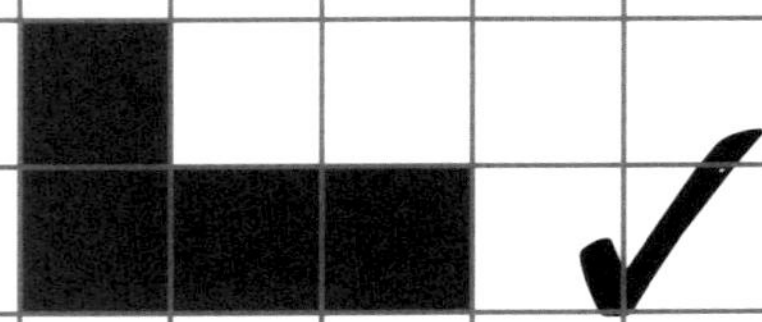

They must not touch just by their corners:

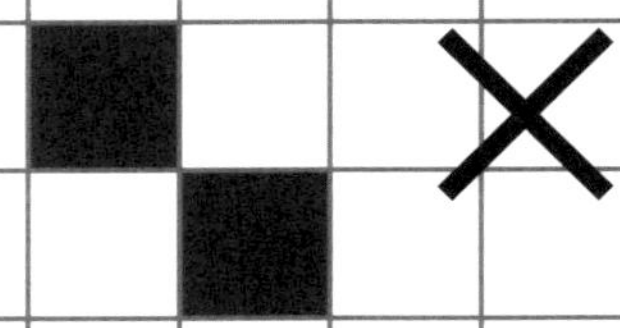

Try to find the longest route across.

Count the number of squares you colour.

Compare your answer to your friend's answer.

The one with most squares in the winner.

Doubling Eric's Wages

Eric helps at home by washing the dishes.

His mum pays him just one penny for doing Monday's dishes!

On Tuesday she doubles his wages, so he gets 2p.

Every day she doubles his wages, compared to the day before.

How much does Eric get paid on Wednesday?

How much does Eric get paid on Thursday?

How much does Eric get paid on Friday?

How much does Eric get paid on Saturday?

How much does Eric get paid on Sunday?

His first week is over. How much has he been paid altogether?

Now he starts his second week.
His mum still keeps doubling his wages.

How much does Eric get paid on Monday?

How much does Eric get paid on Tuesday?

How much does Eric get paid on Wednesday?

How much does Eric get paid on Thursday?

How much does Eric get paid on Friday?

How much does Eric get paid on Saturday?

How much does Eric get paid on Sunday?

How much has Eric been paid altogether for the second week?

Don't forget to help at home without being paid!

Equilateral Triangle Grid

Dotty Equilateral Triangle Grid

10mm Dotty Grid

5mm Grid

10mm Grid